Volume IV:
East Tennessee

Jim Parham

WMC
Publishing

Also by Jim Parham:

OFF THE BEATEN TRACK
Volume I: A Guide to Mountain Biking
in Western North Carolina—
The Smokies

OFF THE BEATEN TRACK
Volume II: A Guide to Mountain Biking
in Western North Carolina—
Pisgah National Forest

OFF THE BEATEN TRACK
Volume III: A Guide to Mountain Biking
in North Georgia

49 Fun & Inexpensive
Things To Do In The Smokies
With Children

WMC Publishing, P.O. Box 158, Almond, N.C. 28702

ISBN 0-9631861-5-9 $12.95
ISSN 1076-6189

Cover design by Ron Roman

A great deal of information is contained in this book and every effort has been made to provide this information as accurately as possible. However, roads and trails can change with time, some roads and trails may not be marked by signs, distances may vary with individual cyclocomputers, and land agency rules and regulations are subject to interpretation and change. There are risks inherent in the sport of mountain biking. *The author and publisher accept no responsibility for inaccuracies or for damages incurred while attempting any of the routes listed.*

Printed in the United States on recycled paper.

A Guide to Mountain Biking in East Tennessee

Volume IV

Jim Parham

TABLE OF CONTENTS

THE TRAILS

INTRODUCTION

East Tennessee has a large variety of terrain awaiting the mountain biker. Along the Tennessee-North Carolina border are the tallest mountains in the state, the Appalachians. In this part of Tennessee, these long, high ridges resemble waves approaching an ocean shore as they ripple down from the state line into the broad Tennessee River Valley. Across this rolling valley to the north rises the Cumberland Plateau—a high, flat sandstone shelf gouged by deep river gorges, the result of years of erosion.

While traveling and biking through east Tennessee, I was amazed at the diversity of trails and bike routes to choose from. All of the land along the Tennessee-North Carolina border and a large section of land on the Cumberland Plateau is in the public domain. For the biker looking for mountain trail riding, this is good news.

Tennessee's Cherokee National Forest stretches all the way from Georgia to Virginia along the North Carolina line. You'll find it's divided into two sections by the Great Smoky Mountains National Park. In both the northern and southern portions the U.S. Forest Service provides many bike riding opportunities. Quite a few trails are specifically designated for mountain bike use and most all of the horse trails, jeep trails and forest roads are open to cyclists as well.

On the Cumberland Plateau, the highest concentration of trails open to mountain bikers is found in the Big South Fork National Recreation Area. Managed by the National Park Service, this area encompasses land in both Tennessee and Kentucky. And unlike most national parks, the Big South Fork National Recreation Area welcomes mountain bikers with open arms. Two single track trails here have been built specifically for bicycle use, the O & W Rail/Trail stretches for over thirty miles, and hundreds of miles of horse trails and jeep roads are all open to cyclists.

In the Tennessee River Valley there are a couple of other areas mountain bikers should know about. Panther Creek State Park, near Morristown, has a trail open to bikers which is great for beginners. The town of Norris, just north of Knoxville, has an entire system of well marked trails and roads which spread out like a spider web across the town's watershed. Many of these are open to bikes.

In this book, I've selected a large assortment of mountain biking routes for you to choose from. If you're getting started as a mountain biker or you just don't like those huffer-puffer hill climbs, take a look at the routes listed in the "easiest trails" section. Most of these are on relatively flat terrain and the distances you'll ride are not too far. If you're a hard core, never-say-die rider, flip toward the back of the book to the "most difficult trails" section. Here you'll find rides with elements ranging from long, strenuous climbs, to very technical sections, to steep, stone-staircase descents. And of course, for those of you who fall somewhere between these two extremes, look to the larger, "more difficult trails" section for a good general mix of exciting and fun routes.

Interesting rides are available regardless of the weather or the time of year. East Tennessee experiences relatively mild winters with little snowfall—in fact, you can ride here year-round. If it's wet and rainy outside, I suggest staying off the single track trails and heading for the gravel road loops. This saves a lot of wear and tear on both you and your equipment, as well as on the trail. If the Appalachians are socked in with bad weather, you may find it's sunny and clear up on the Plateau. Or it may be the other way around.

If you haven't used one of these guides before, study the "How To Use This Book" section well before you head out on the trail. This will make the maps and directions that follow easier to understand. I've also included information on mountain bike etiquette and riding on Tennessee's public lands. Mountain bikers are the fastest growing and newest group of users in the woods and following these guidelines can only help advance our sport.

The last section of this book holds regional information resources for bikers, lodging, camping and weather. If you are visiting Tennessee from afar and plan to stay overnight or for an entire vacation, the information here should help you out.

East Tennessee offers some very fine mountain biking. Whether touring the plateaus of the Big South Fork National Recreation Area, riding from fire tower to fire tower in the Appalachians, or rolling along in the Tennessee River Valley in between, I've found the eastern end of the state a real pleasure for cycling. With the aid of this book, it's my hope that you will too.

JP
November, 1994

How To Use This Book

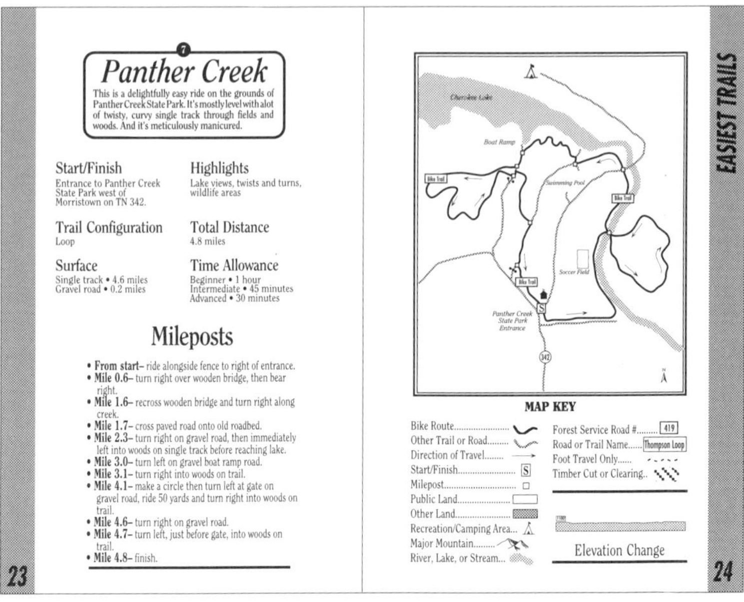

Typical Route Description Page

- The **route number** appears in a circle, square, or diamond at the top of the left hand page. The number corresponds to the route number in the table of contents, and the circle (easiest), square (more difficult), or diamond (most difficult) indicates the route difficulty.

- **Route difficulty** (also shown vertically at the edge of the top right hand corner of the right page) is relative to this book and the Tennessee mountains. Some trails pass through extreme mountainous terrain. Others are in low, rolling valleys. You can expect to find difficulties of every kind, including long, steep uphills and downhills, stream crossings, sand pits, and plenty of narrow, technical single track.

- Below the **route name** is a brief description of the route's more noted highlights.

- **Start/Finish** indicates where the route begins and how to get there.

- **Trail Configuration** describes the type of route.

- There are three **Surface** types: single track, gravel road, and pavement. This shows how many miles to expect of each surface.

"""

- In the **Highlights** there will be a one- or two-word description of things you can expect on the trail. For example, *sand pits* means: there are areas of deep, unavoidable sand on the trail. Sand is tough to ride through and accelerates wear and tear on your bike.

- The **Total Distance** shows the number of miles you will travel.

- **Time Allowance** is a rough approximation of the time it will take you to ride the trail with *minimal* stops according to your ability level.

- Each **Milepost** corresponds to the adjoining map. The first milepost is at the Start/Finish and is represented by a ⑤ on the map. There is a milepost for every turn or any other place of note and each is represented by a □ on the map.

- The **maps** are oriented north with all roads or trails marked by name or number.   All roads, trails, buildings, clearings, and other features relevant to the route are shown, as well as the best direction of travel. Some of the routes listed in this book can be linked together for shorter or longer rides. When this is the case, those trails or roads are also shown on the map. However, no mileposts or directions are given for these combined rides. **Maps are not drawn to scale.**

- The **Map Key** shows what each symbol represents as well as indicating the shading used for different types of trails, roads, or land. The main route is always shown in black.

- By looking at the **Elevation Change**, you can get a pretty good idea where the major hills are in the route, how long they will be, and the degree of steepness. It does not show every short rise or dip in the trail.

Other Sections

- There are two sections immediately following this page that cover **Mountain Bike Etiquette** and **Riding On East Tennessee's Public Lands**. Knowing and following the rules and using good judgement is critical in keeping public land accessible to mountain bikers.

- On the **Orientation Pages** you'll find a map showing where the riding region is as it relates to the rest of Tennessee and an area map indicating where you'll find the start/finish for each route.

- In the **Regional Information** section are several subsections that provide information on places to stay in the area, where bike shops are located, and what kind of weather and temperatures you can expect at different times of the year.

Mountain Bike Etiquette

The old phrase "use it or lose it" has never been more true than in the case of mountain biking on public and private lands. In this case it's more appropriate to say "use it *properly* or lose it." It takes only a few incidences of irresponsible or abusive trail riding to close a trail, a recreation area, or an entire national forest to mountain bikers. Below is a list of guidelines to follow while on the trail.

- Ride only on roads and trails authorized for mountain bike use. Some trails and areas do not permit mountain bike use at all.

- To avoid trail erosion, carry your bike over wet and boggy areas, stepping stones, and steps. Also avoid skidding or spinning out on steep grades.

- Control your speed and approach turns in anticipation of someone around the bend.

- Always wear your helmet.

- Pack out what you pack in.

- Follow the directions of the "yield to" sign shown below. Dismount and be courteous to all other trail users when approaching from behind or ahead and make your presence known well in advance. If you meet horseback riders, speak out in a normal voice while they pass. This calms both the horses and their riders.

Riding on East Tennessee's Public Lands

Tennessee is full of public land agencies, each with its own set of rules regarding trails and mountain bike use. The routes in this book cross lands in the Cherokee National Forest, the Big South Fork National Recreation Area, Panther Creek State Park and the City of Norris. All of the routes in this book are currently open to mountain bike use.

Cherokee National Forest

The Cherokee National Forest is divided in half by the Great Smoky Mountains National Park. The two sections lie along the North Carolina border—one south and one north of the Park. Each section is divided into ranger districts and each district has a good number of roads and trails open to mountain bikes. Here are the rules: All hiking/foot trails are closed to bikes. Designated bike trails, motorcycle trails, ATV and ORV trails, horse trails, gated roads and any other roads are open to bikes unless signs are posted that say otherwise.

Big South Fork National Recreation Area

The Big South Fork is managed by the National Park Service and is one of the United States' newest national recreation areas. Within it, two trails have been built specifically for mountain bike use. Cyclists also have over 150 miles of horse trails and gravel and 4-wheel drive roads to choose from. Bikes are not allowed on hiking trails and there is an area-wide bike speed limit of 25 mph.

City of Norris

The Norris watershed, an area located just north of Norris, Tennessee, is laced with both foot trails and multiuse trails and roads. Mountain bikes are allowed on all the multiuse trails—these are marked with purple signs—and any of the roads. Bikes are not allowed on the foot trails; these are marked with red signs.

Panther Creek State Park

At present the bike trail at Panther Creek State Park is simply known as "the bike trail" and it is the only trail open to bikes in the Park.

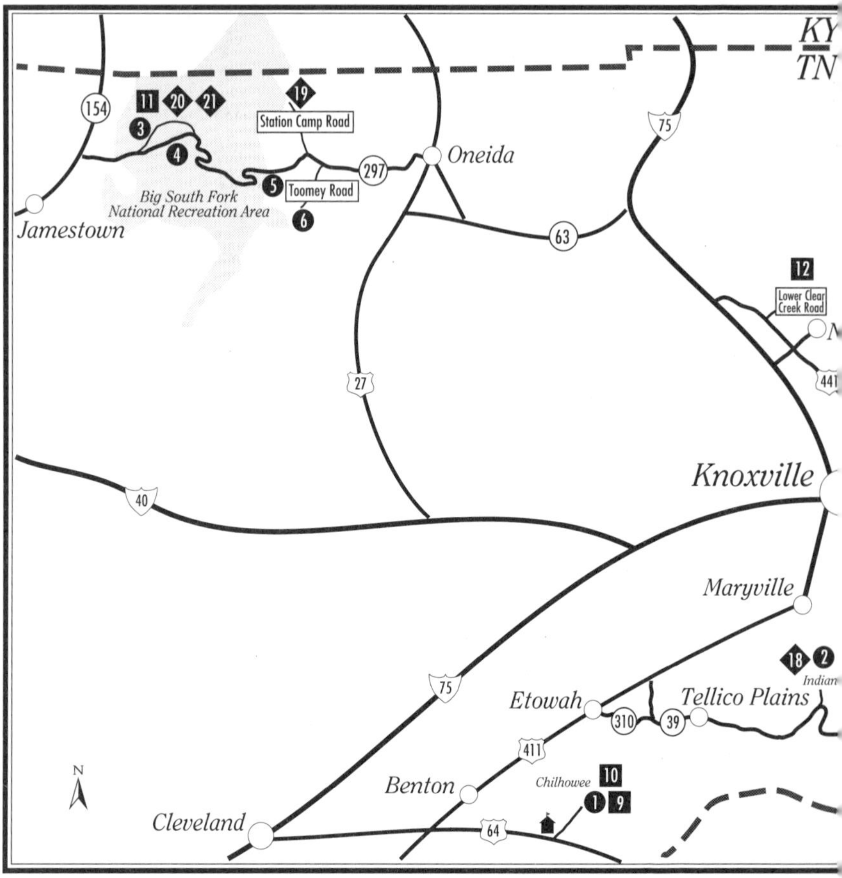

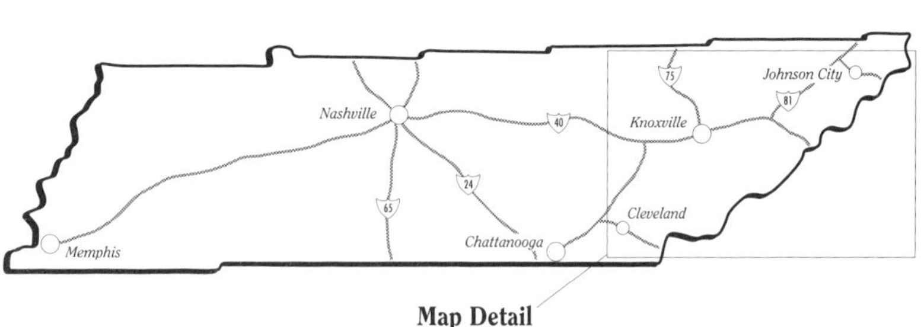

Map Detail

Orientation Map

● Easiest Trails

1– Benton Falls
2– Indian Boundary
3– Collier Ridge
4– Leatherwood
5– O & W Overlook
6– O & W Railroad
7– Panther Creek
8– Flatwoods

■ More Difficult Trails

9– Clemmer
10– Oswald Dome
11– Duncan Hollow
12– Norris

13– Chimney Rocks
14– Paint Rock
15– Poplar Cove
16– Buffalo Mountain
17– Pinnacle Tower

◆ Most Difficult Trails

18– Citico Creek
19– Big Island
20– Charit Creek Lodge
21– North White Oak
22– Hurrican Gap
23– Viking Mountain
24– Horse Creek
25– McQueen Gap

EASIEST TRAILS

1– Benton Falls • 3 Miles
2– Indian Boundary • 3.2 Miles
3– Collier Ridge • 7.5 Miles
4– Leatherwood • 5.2 Miles
5– O & W Overlook • 1.6 Miles
6– O & W Railroad • 22.4 Miles
7– Panther Creek • 4.8 Miles
8– Flatwoods • 18.1 Miles

Benton Falls

If you're just getting started in the sport, this route is a great introduction to single track riding. If you've been biking awhile, you'll love its simplicity. The trail takes you out to Benton Falls and the head of the Rock Creek Scenic Gorge along the top of Chilhowee Mountain.

Start/Finish

Chilhowee Recreation Area Picnic Parking Lot 7 miles off US 64 east of Benton. If the recreation area is closed, start at the entrance gate.

Trail Configuration

Loop with extension

Surface

Single track • 2.5 miles
Pavement • 0.5 miles

Highlights

Designated bike trail, roots, lake, waterfall, campground

Total Distance

3 miles

Time Allowance

Beginner • 1 hour
Intermediate • 45 minutes
Advanced • 30 minutes

Mileposts

- **From start**– ride out past picnic area below dam on Benton Falls Trail (**blue blazes**).
- **Mile 1.1**– Red Leaf Trail enters from left. Continue to Benton Falls on Benton Falls Trail.
- **Mile 1.4**– Benton Falls. Leave your bike here. It's a short hike to the falls, then turn around.
- **Mile 1.7**– turn right on Red Leaf Trail (**red blazes**).
- **Mile 1.9**– turn right on Arbutus Trail (**orange blazes**).
- **Mile 2.2**– Clear Creek Trail exits to the right and then the Azalea Trail exits to the right. Bear left each time.
- **Mile 2.3**– turn right on Azalea Trail (**yellow blazes**).
- **Mile 2.5**– campground. Turn left.
- **Mile 3**– finish.

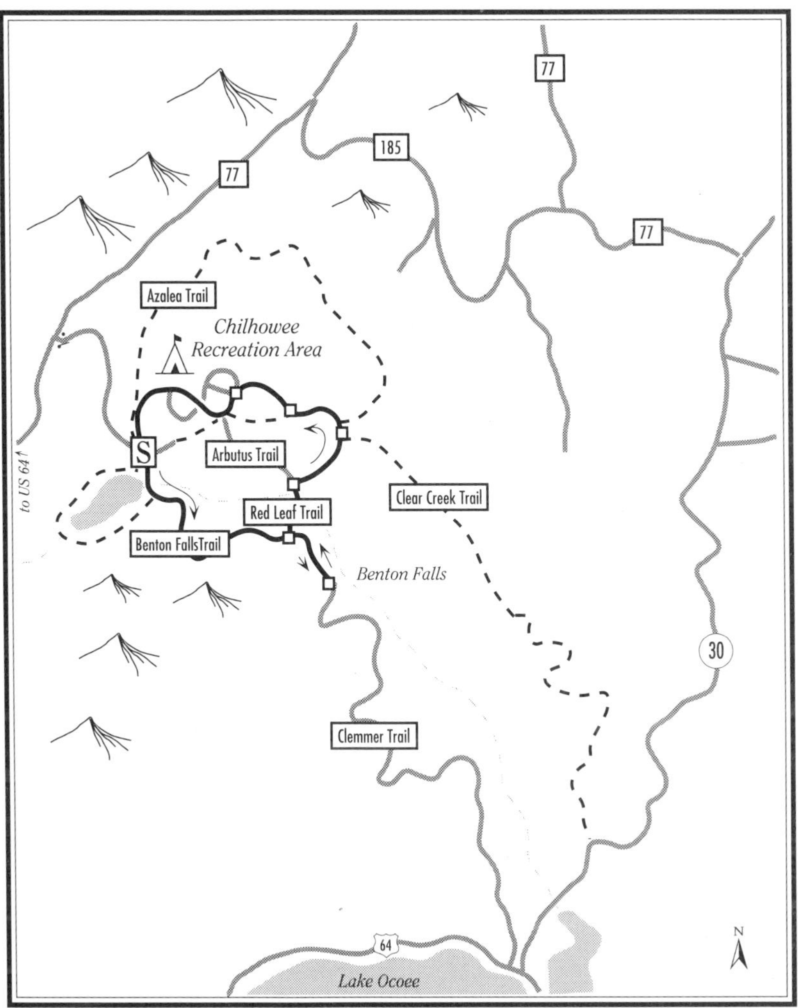

MAP KEY

Bike Route.........................

Other Trail or Road..........

Direction of Travel...............

Start/Finish........................... S

Milepost......................................

Public Land.......................

Other Land.......................

Recreation/Camping Area....

Major Mountain........

River, Lake, or Stream.....

Forest Service Rd. #................. 419

Road or Trail Name...... Thompson Loop

Foot Travel Only.............

Timber Cut or Clearing..

1880'
1720'

Elevation Change

Indian Boundary

This is the ideal beginner ride. It's all smooth, lightly-graveled single track. It's level, has bridges across all the streams, and completely encircles a high mountain lake. The views of the surrounding Unicoi Mountains are spectacular, and there's even a bath house at the trailhead.

Start/Finish

Indian Boundary Recreation Area Swimming Beach, north of Tellico Plains on TN 165.

Trail Configuration

Loop

Surface

Single track • 3.2 miles

Highlights

Lake and mountain views, excellent riding surface, bridges

Total Distance

3.2 miles

Time Allowance

Beginner • 1 hour
Intermediate • 30 minutes
Advanced • 20 minutes

Mileposts

- **From start–** ride clockwise on bike trail at edge of lake out past the campground and boat launching area.
- **Mile 1.6–** woods road enters from the left.
- **Mile 1.7–** woods road exits to the left.
- **Mile 2.5–** woods road enters from the left, follows trail a short distance and then exits to the left.
- **Mile 3–** cross dam and spillway, then bear right on trail.
- **Mile 3.2–** finish.

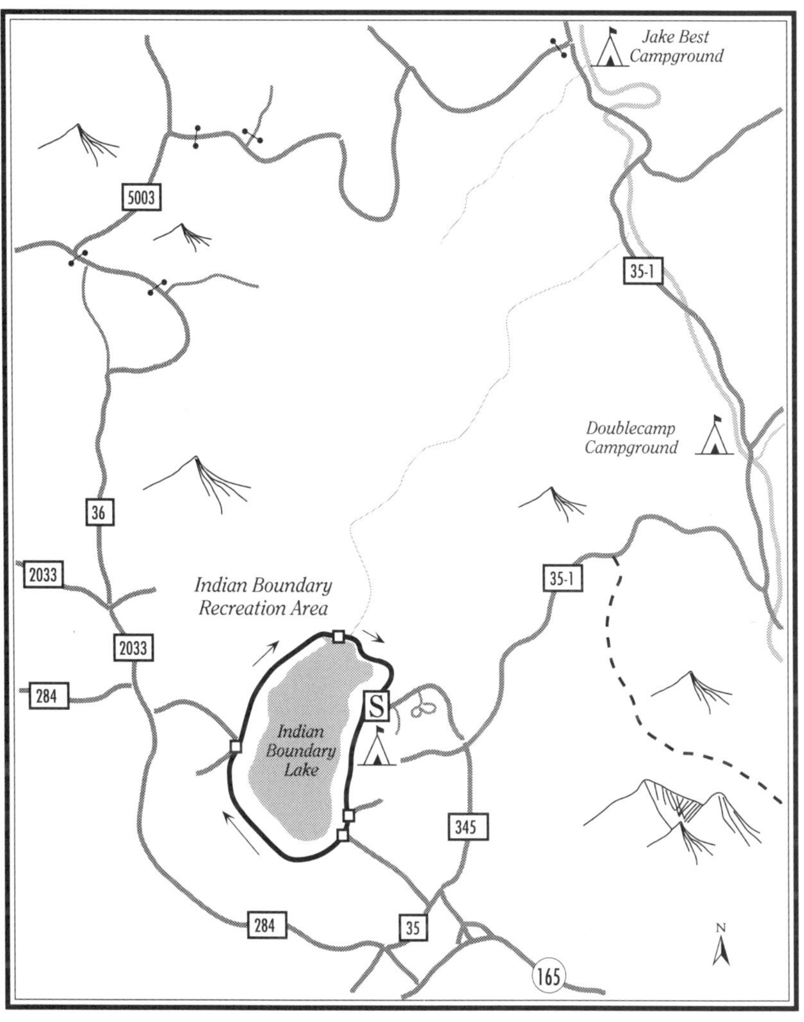

MAP KEY

Bike Route......................

Other Trail or Road...........

Direction of Travel............... →

Start/Finish........................... S

Milepost............................... □

Public Land....................

Other Land......................

Recreation/Camping Area....

Major Mountain........

River, Lake, or Stream.....

Forest Service Rd. #.................. 419

Road or Trail Name...... Thompson Loop

Foot Travel Only.............

Timber Cut or Clearing..

1760'

Elevation Change

Collier Ridge

Built specifically for mountain bikers, this trail winds through the woods of the Big South Fork National Recreation Area near Bandy Creek Campground. You'll find smooth single track with one really fun twisty, curvy downhill.

Start/Finish

Bandy Creek Campground, Big South Fork National Recreation Area west of Oneida off TN 297.

Trail Configuration

Loop with extension

Surface

Single track • 4.2 miles
Gravel road • 1.6 miles
Pavement • 1.7 miles

Highlights

Small stream crossings, sandy spots, well marked, short hills, big flat rocks, mud holes

Total Distance

7.5 miles

Time Allowance

Beginner • 1.75 hours
Intermediate • 1.25 hours
Advanced • 45 minutes

Mileposts

- **From start**– ride west out Bandy Creek Road.
- **Mile 1.0**– turn left on Collier Ridge Bike Trail. It's marked by a wooden post with **orange** letters.
- **Mile 1.3**– just after crossing the creek a hiking trail joins the bike trail and then the bike trail splits. Bear left to start the loop. You'll finish by riding down the right fork.
- **Mile 1.9**– hiking trail exits to the left. Bear right.
- **Mile 2.9**– turn right on TN 297.
- **Mile 4.2**– turn right on bike trail.
- **Mile 4.3**– hiker trail enters from left. Bear right.
- **Mile 4.6**– hiker trail exits to right. Bear left.
- **Mile 6.2**– bottom of downhill and end of loop. Turn left.
- **Mile 6.5**– turn right on Bandy Creek Road.
- **Mile 7.5**– finish.

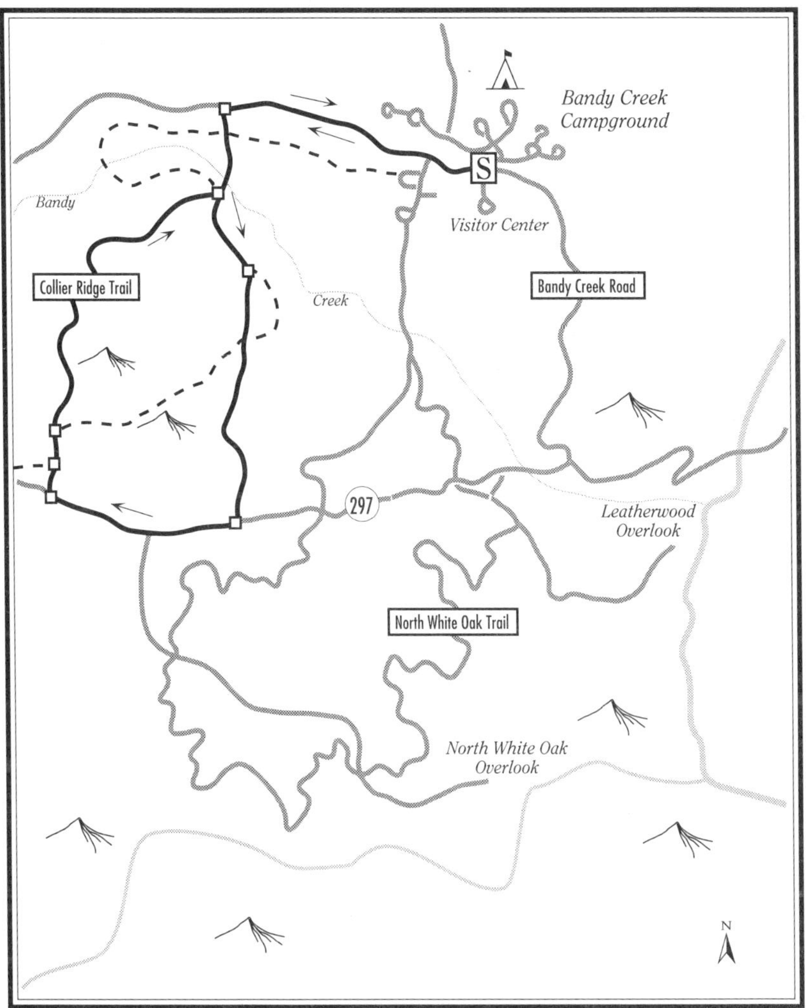

MAP KEY

Bike Route......................		Forest Service Rd. #..................	419
Other Trail or Road...........		Road or Trail Name......	Thompson Loop
Direction of Travel................	→	Foot Travel Only.............	
Start/Finish...........................	S	Timber Cut or Clearing..	
Milepost................................	□		
Public Land......................			
Other Land......................			
Recreation/Camping Area....			
Major Mountain........		1600'	
River, Lake, or Stream.....		1420'	

Elevation Change

4

Leatherwood

Tennessee Highway 297 crosses the Big South Fork at Leatherwood Ford. Atop the cliffs, high above the river, sits an overlook. If you've got a keen eye, you can see it as you cross the bridge in your car. You'll ride there on this easy route.

Start/Finish

On TN 297, 1.5 miles west of the entrance to Bandy Creek Campground in the Big South Fork National Recreation Area near Oneida. A horse trail crosses here.

Trail Configuration

Out-and-back

Surface

Single track/4WD • 5.2 miles

Highlights

Horse use, 4WD use, sand, good views, large field crossing, a somewhat level ride

Total Distance

5.2 miles

Time Allowance

Beginner • 1 hour
Intermediate • 45 minutes
Advanced • 30 minutes

Mileposts

- **From start**– ride out Leatherwood Road.
- **Mile 0.1**– bear right on sandy road bed.
- **Mile 0.7**– North White Oak Horse Trail enters from the right.
- **Mile 1.1**– road forks; bear left.
- **Mile 2.1**– after crossing large field, bear left at fork.
- **Mile 2.6**– turn around area. It's a short hike from here to the overlook. Return the way you came.
- **Mile 5.2**– finish.

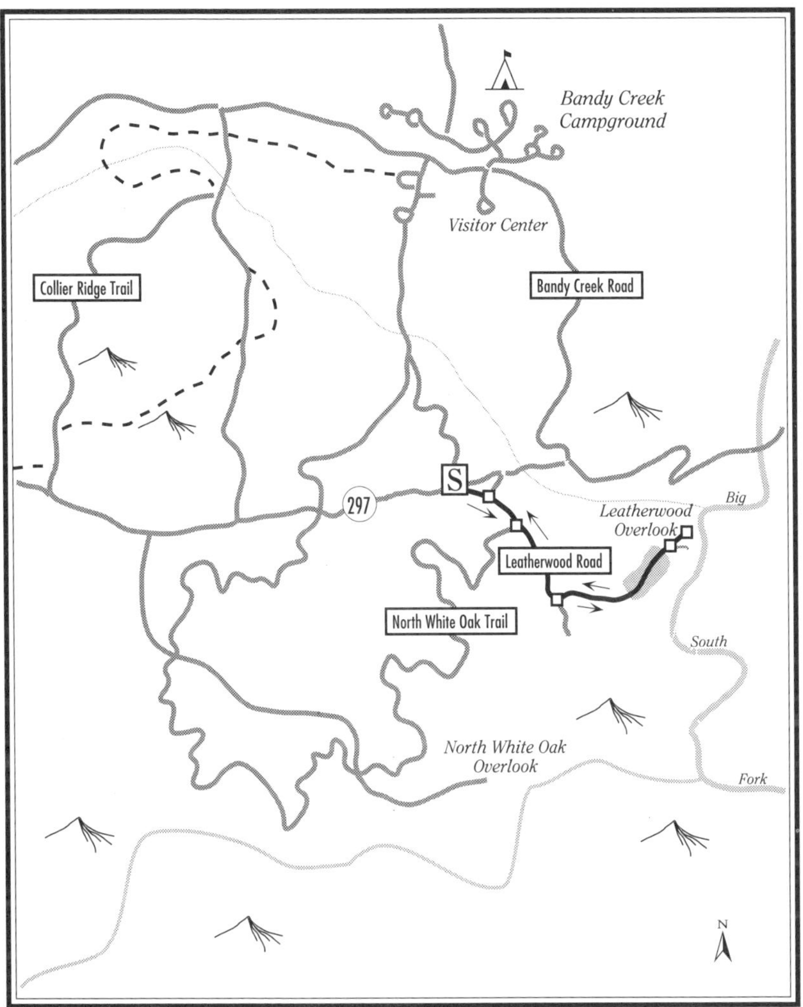

MAP KEY

Bike Route......................

Other Trail or Road...........

Direction of Travel................

Start/Finish...................... S

Milepost.............................. □

Public Land......................

Other Land......................

Recreation/Camping Area....

Major Mountain........

River, Lake, or Stream.....

Forest Service Rd. #.................. 419

Road or Trail Name...... Thompson Loop

Foot Travel Only.............

Timber Cut or Clearing..

1500'

Elevation Change

5

O & W Overlook

This short ride out to the O & W Railroad Bridge Overlook is great for beginners or anyone looking for a fine clifftop view. The old 4WD road rolls gently out to the very brink of the Big South Fork Gorge. Be very careful as you near the edge; there's no guard rail on this one.

Start/Finish

On TN 297, just past the eastern entrance sign to the Big South Fork National Recreation Area. The 4WD road starts on the south side of the highway next to the speed limit sign.

Trail Configuration

Out-and-back

Surface

Single track/4WD • 1.6 miles

Highlights

4WD use, spectacular views, mud holes, slight hills

Total Distance

1.6 miles

Time Allowance

Beginner • 45 minutes
Intermediate • 30 minutes
Advanced • 20 minutes

Mileposts

- **From start–** ride out O & W Overlook Road (it's unmarked).
- **Mile 0.8–** turn around area. It's a short hike from here to the overlook. Be very careful at the cliff's edge. Return the way you came.
- **Mile 1.6–** finish.

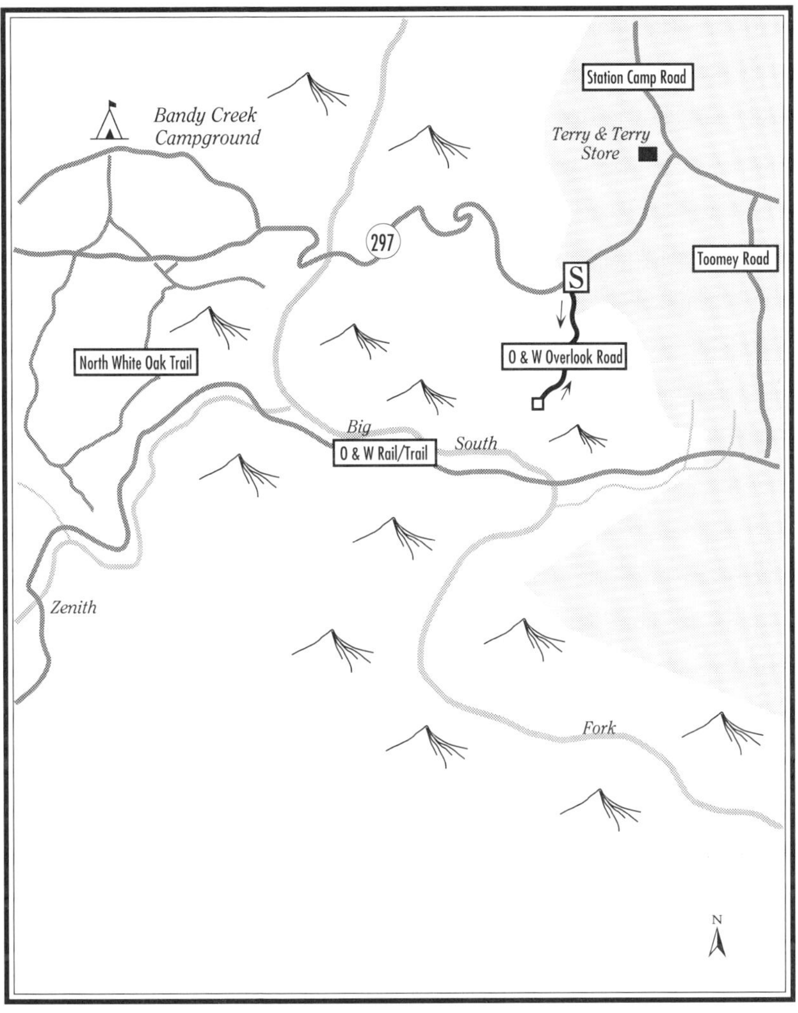

MAP KEY

Bike Route......................	Forest Service Rd. #................. 419
Other Trail or Road..........	Road or Trail Name...... Thompson Loop
Direction of Travel................ →	Foot Travel Only.............
Start/Finish........................... S	Timber Cut or Clearing..
Milepost................................ □	
Public Land.....................	
Other Land.....................	
Recreation/Camping Area....	1500'
Major Mountain........	
River, Lake, or Stream.....	**Elevation Change**

6

O & W Railroad

A must ride if you're visiting the Big South Fork National Recreational Area. This level rail/trail route takes you into the Big South Fork Gorge, across the river on a high tressle, and alongside the rapids of North White Oak Creek to Zenith. If it's cold or you want to keep your feet dry, turn around at the first stream crossing. If you continue on, plan to get both wet and muddy.

Start/Finish

From Terry and Terry Store on TN 297 drive towards Oneida 0.6 miles and turn right on unmarked Toomey Road. Drive 2.4 miles to rail/trail. It looks like a gravel road at the start.

Trail Configuration

Out-and-back

Surface

4WD • 22.4 miles

Highlights

4WD use, trestles, huge mud holes, stream crossings, views

Total Distance

22.4 miles

Time Allowance

Beginner • 4 hours
Intermediate • 3 hours
Advanced • 2 hours

Mileposts

- **From start–** ride over first trestle and out rail/trail.
- **Mile 4.1–** high trestle over Big South Fork of the Cumberland River.
- **Mile 5.4–** ford North White Oak Creek.
- **Mile 9.5–** road enters from right. Ford stream and bear left on rail/trail.
- **Mile 11.2–** Zenith. This is a boat launch area. There is no need to ford the stream. Turn around here and return the way you came.
- **Mile 22.4–** finish.

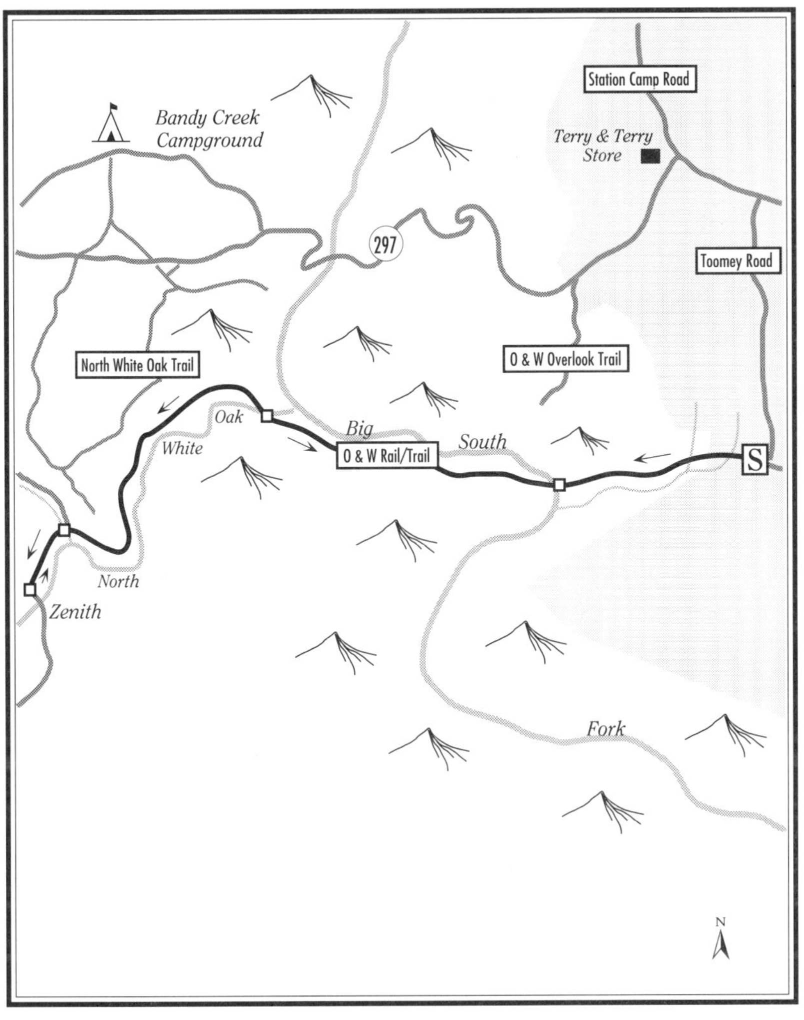

MAP KEY

Bike Route......................		Forest Service Rd. #................	419
Other Trail or Road...........		Road or Trail Name......	Thompson Loop
Direction of Travel................	→	Foot Travel Only.............	
Start/Finish............................	S	Timber Cut or Clearing..	
Milepost..................................	□		
Public Land......................			
Other Land......................			
Recreation/Camping Area....			
Major Mountain........			
River, Lake, or Stream.....			

900'

Elevation Change

(7)

Panther Creek

This is a delightfully easy ride on the grounds of Panther Creek State Park. It's mostly level with a lot of twisty, curvy single track through fields and woods. And it's meticulously manicured.

Start/Finish

Entrance to Panther Creek State Park west of Morristown on TN 342.

Trail Configuration

Loop

Surface

Single track • 4.6 miles
Gravel road • 0.2 miles

Highlights

Lake views, twists and turns, wildlife areas

Total Distance

4.8 miles

Time Allowance

Beginner • 1 hour
Intermediate • 45 minutes
Advanced • 30 minutes

Mileposts

- **From start**– ride alongside fence to right of entrance.
- **Mile 0.6**– turn right over wooden bridge, then bear right.
- **Mile 1.6**– recross wooden bridge and turn right along creek.
- **Mile 1.7**– cross paved road onto old roadbed.
- **Mile 2.3**– turn right on gravel road, then immediately left into woods on single track before reaching lake.
- **Mile 3.0**– turn left on gravel boat ramp road.
- **Mile 3.1**– turn right into woods on trail.
- **Mile 4.1**– make a circle then turn left at gate on gravel road, ride 50 yards and turn right into woods on trail.
- **Mile 4.6**– turn right on gravel road.
- **Mile 4.7**– turn left, just before gate, into woods on trail.
- **Mile 4.8**– finish.

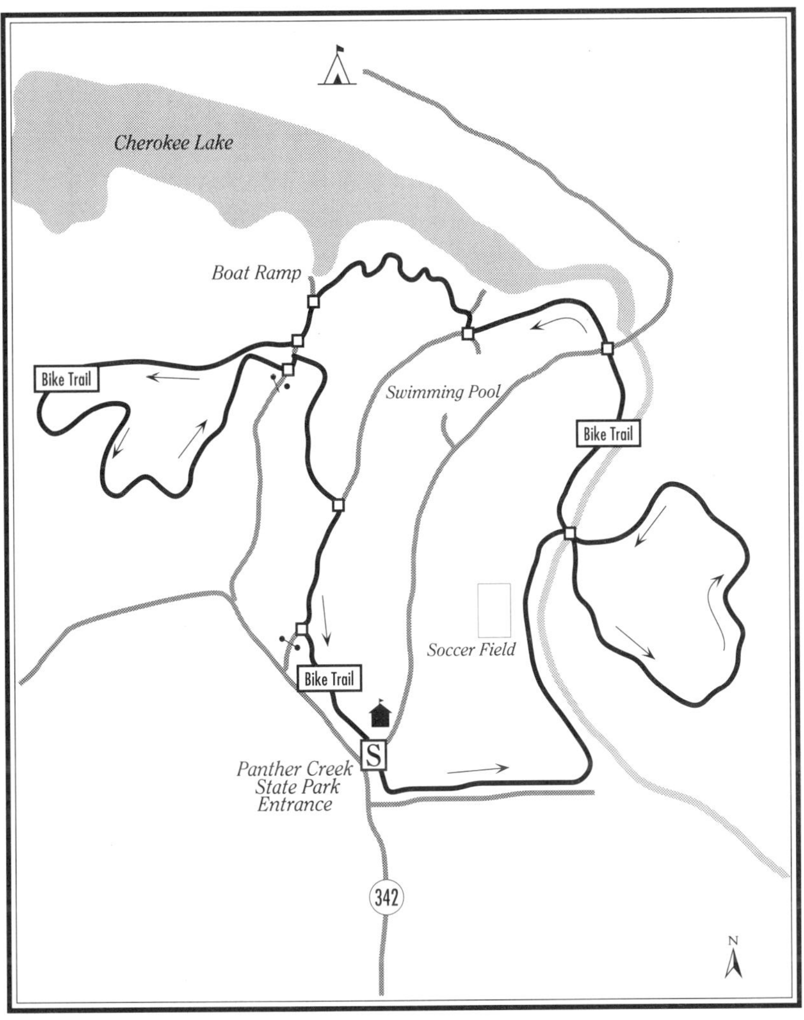

MAP KEY

Bike Route.........................

Other Trail or Road...........

Direction of Travel...............

Start/Finish.......................... S

Milepost.............................. □

Public Land......................

Other Land......................

Recreation/Camping Area....

Major Mountain........

River, Lake, or Stream.....

Forest Service Rd. #.................. 419

Road or Trail Name...... Thompson Loop

Foot Travel Only............

Timber Cut or Clearing..

1100'

Elevation Change

⑧ *Flatwoods*

The Flatwoods, squeezed between Holston Mountain and Holston Lake, are only somewhat flat. This route rolls along the edge of the mountain, making use of two gated forest service roads before returning alongside the lake. This is a good wet weather alternative.

Start/Finish

From Bristol, take US 421 south 12 miles to Camp Tom Howard Road (FS 87). Turn right and drive 1 mile to gated FS 87B. Start here.

Trail Configuration

Loop

Surface

Single track • 0.5 miles
Gravel road • 17.6 miles

Highlights

Horse use, views of mountains and lake, wildlife areas, short rocky section

Total Distance

18.1 miles

Time Allowance

Beginner • 3 hours
Intermediate • 2.25 hours
Advanced • 1.75 hours

Mileposts

- **From start**– ride around gate and up FS 87B. It's signed as trail # 46 and marked with **yellow blazes**.
- **Mile 5.1**– turn left onto single track. Follow blazes and sign.
- **Mile 5.6**– turn left on FS 87A.
- **Mile 9.1**– trail # 46 exits road to left. (It continues for another 5.5 miles to FS 87, but is unsuitable for bikes.) Stay on FS 87A.
- **Mile 9.4**– ride around gate and turn right on FS 87.
- **Mile 18.1**– finish.

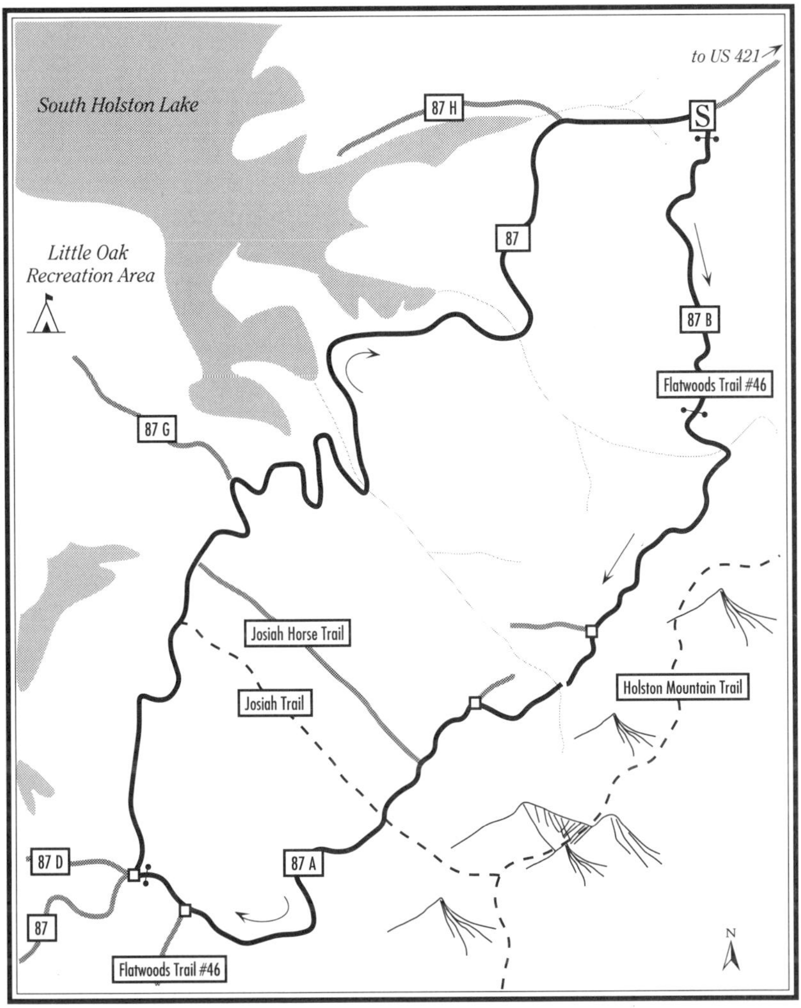

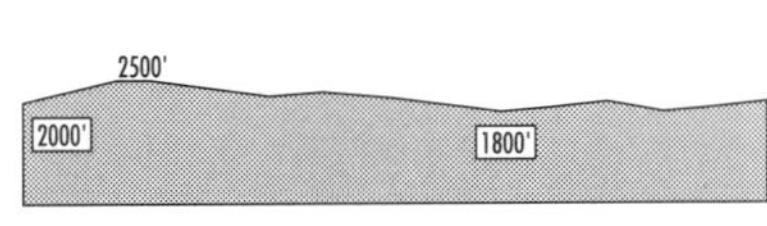

South Holston Lake

Little Oak
Recreation Area

to US 421

87 H

87

87 B

Flatwoods Trail #46

87 G

Josiah Horse Trail

Josiah Trail

Holston Mountain Trail

87 D

87 A

87

Flatwoods Trail #46

N

MAP KEY

Bike Route.....................

Other Trail or Road...........

Direction of Travel...............

Start/Finish.......................... S

Milepost.................................

Public Land.....................

Other Land......................

Recreation/Camping Area....

Major Mountain........

River, Lake, or Stream.....

Forest Service Rd. #................. 419

Road or Trail Name...... Thompson Loop

Foot Travel Only.............

Timber Cut or Clearing..

2500'

2000'   1800'

Elevation Change

MORE DIFFICULT TRAILS

9– Clemmer • 20.6 Miles
10– Oswald Dome • 16.4 Miles
11– Duncan Hollow • 4.6 Miles
12– Norris • 8.6 Miles
13– Chimney Rocks • 13.5 Miles
14– Paint Rock • 13.6 Miles
15– Poplar Cove • 5 Miles
16– Buffalo Mountain • 6.6 Miles
17– Pinnacle Tower • 12.5 Miles

Clemmer

This designated bike trail might well be called *clinger,* as it literally clings to the side of Rock Creek Gorge on its descent to Lake Ocoee. After a pleasant roll through the Greasy Creek Community, a steady climb brings you back on top of Chilhowee Mountain on a gravel road.

Start/Finish

Chilhowee Recreation Area Picnic Parking Lot off US 64 east of Benton. *An alternate start is located at the jct. of US 64 and TN 30.*

Trail Configuration

Loop

Surface

Single track • 5.9 miles
Gravel road • 7.9 miles
Pavement • 6.8 miles

Highlights

Good views, roots, lake, waterfall, stream crossings, rocks, valley

Total Distance

20.6 miles

Time Allowance

Beginner • 4.5 hours
Intermediate • 3 hours
Advanced • 2 hours

Mileposts

- **From start**– ride out past picnic area below dam on Benton Falls Trail (**blue blazes**).
- **Mile 1.1**– Red Leaf Trail enters from left. Continue to Benton Falls on Benton Falls Trail.
- **Mile 1.4**– Benton Falls. It's a short hike to the falls, then continue on Clemmer Trail (**cream blazes**).
- **Mile 4.8**– turn left on FS 33101.
- **Mile 5.9**– turn left on US 64 then left on TN 30.
- **Mile 12.2**– turn left on FS 77.
- **Mile 14.2**– turn left on FS 185.
- **Mile 18.1**– turn left on FS 77.
- **Mile 20.1**– turn left toward Chilhowee Campground.
- **Mile 20.6**– finish.

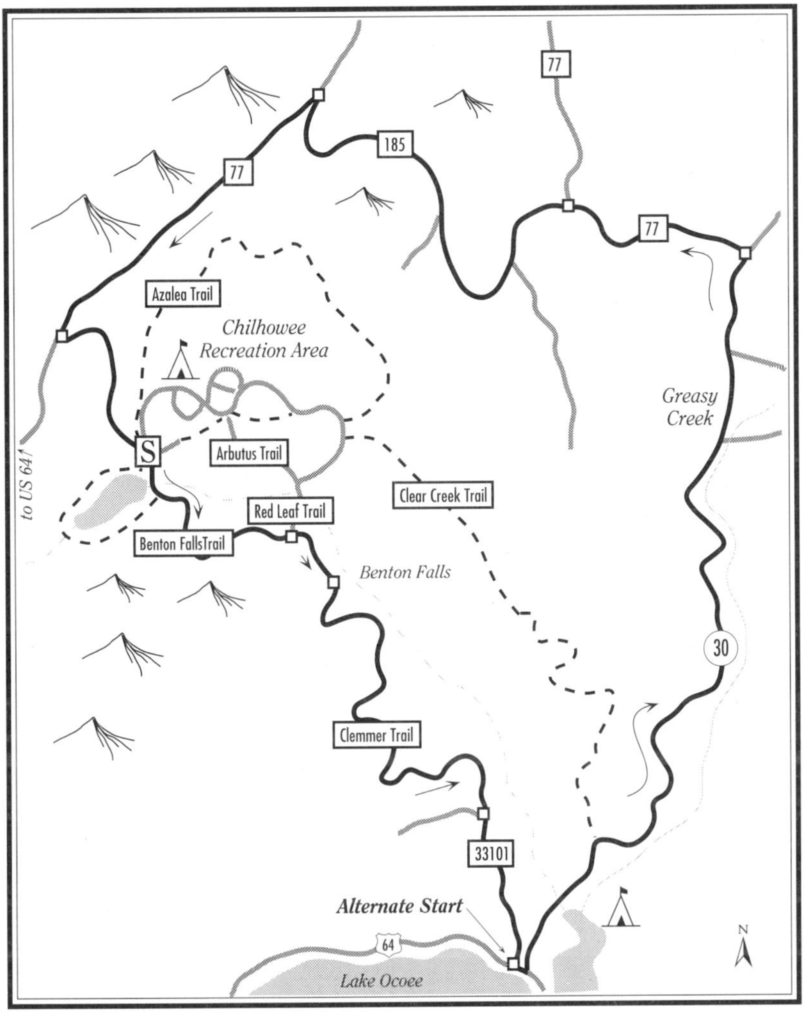

MAP KEY

Bike Route.......................

Other Trail or Road..........

Direction of Travel...............

Start/Finish............................ **S**

Milepost.................................

Public Land........................

Other Land.......................

Recreation/Camping Area....

Major Mountain........

River, Lake, or Stream.....

Forest Service Rd. #................. 419

Road or Trail Name...... Thompson Loop

Foot Travel Only.............

Timber Cut or Clearing..

Elevation Change

Oswald Dome

10

Starting with a short climb and then six miles of downhill, the first half of this ride goes by fast. Don't get too carried away; it's a solid four-and-a-half-mile climb to the lookout tower. You'll complete the ride along the spine of Chilhowee Mountain where good views await.

Start/Finish

Chilhowee Recreation Area Picnic Parking Lot off US 64 east of Benton. If the recreation area is closed, start at the entrance gate.

Trail Configuration

Loop with extensions

Surface

Gravel road • 15.4 miles
Pavement • 1 mile

Highlights

Lookout tower, long hills, great views of two valleys

Total Distance

16.4 miles

Time Allowance

Beginner • 3.5 hours
Intermediate • 2.25 hours
Advanced • 1.5 hours

Mileposts

- **From start–** ride up paved campground entrance road.
- **Mile 0.5–** turn right on FS 77.
- **Mile 2.5–** turn right on FS 185.
- **Mile 6.4–** end of downhill. Turn left on FS 77.
- **Mile 9.8–** FS 77 continues to left. Bear right up Oswald Dome Road.
- **Mile 10.8–** lookout tower. Turn around here.
- **Mile 11.8–** turn right on FS 77.
- **Mile 13.8–** FS 185 enters from left. Continue on FS 77.
- **Mile 15.9–** turn left into campground.
- **Mile 16.4–** finish.

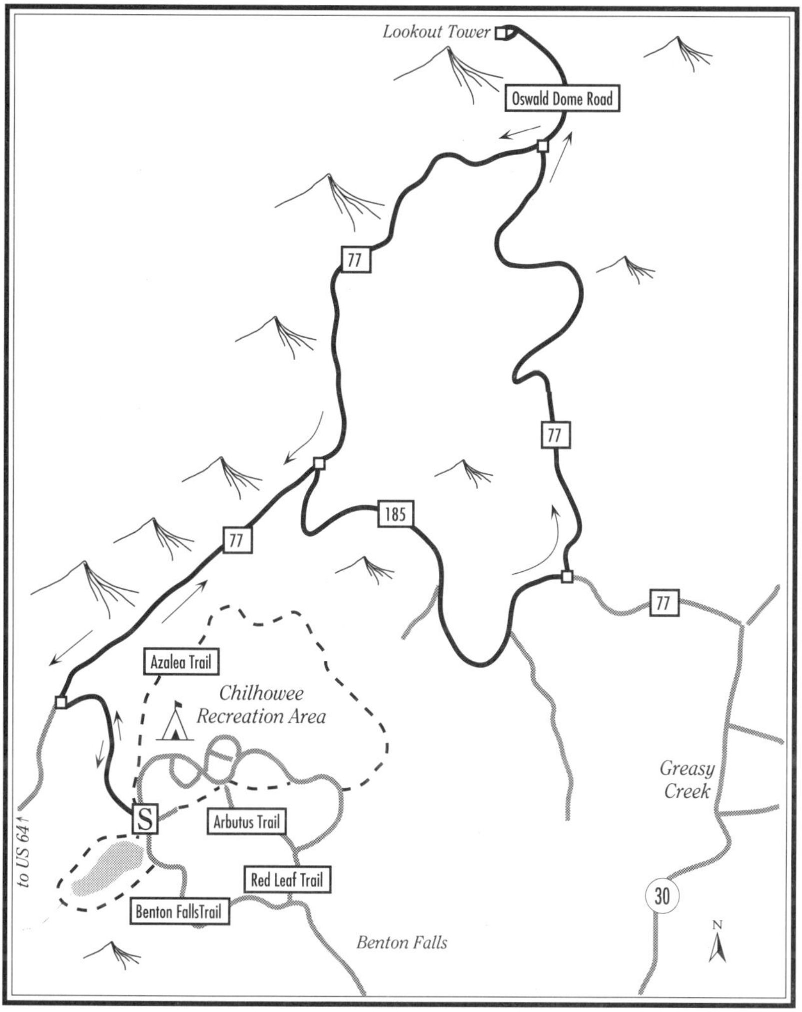

MAP KEY

Bike Route.........................

Other Trail or Road..........

Direction of Travel...............

Start/Finish............................ $\boxed{S}$

Milepost....................................

Public Land.......................

Other Land.......................

Recreation/Camping Area....

Major Mountain........

River, Lake, or Stream.....

Forest Service Rd. #.................. $\boxed{419}$

Road or Trail Name...... $\boxed{\text{Thompson Loop}}$

Foot Travel Only.............

Timber Cut or Clearing..

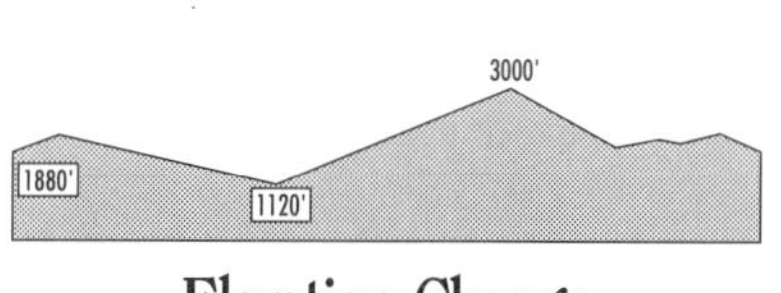

Elevation Change

Duncan Hollow

This woods loop designated for mountain bikers combines single track with 4WD roads for a technical, exciting ride. On one downhill you'll roll down a natural sandstone staircase, and the stream crossing will really test your riding skills.

Start/Finish

Bandy Creek Swimming Pool, Big South Fork National Recreation Area west of Oneida off TN 297.

Trail Configuration

Loop with extension

Surface

Single track/4WD • 2.4 miles
Gravel road • 2.2 miles

Highlights

Small stream crossing, sandy spots, well marked, short hills, big rocks, mud holes, some horse use

Total Distance

4.6 miles

Time Allowance

Beginner • 1 hour
Intermediate • 45 minutes
Advanced • 30 minutes

Mileposts

- **From start–** ride down Duncan Hollow Road. There is a post here with "bicycles" written in **orange** letters.
- **Mile 0.8–** power lines cross trail. A short section of bike trail exits and then reenters Duncan Hollow Road.
- **Mile 1.1–** turn left on By Pass Road.
- **Mile 1.3–** bike trail enters from right. Bear left to start the loop.
- **Mile 1.7–** turn right off road onto bike trail.
- **Mile 3.2–** end of loop. Turn left on By Pass Road.
- **Mile 3.5–** turn right on Duncan Hollow Road.
- **Mile 4.6–** finish.

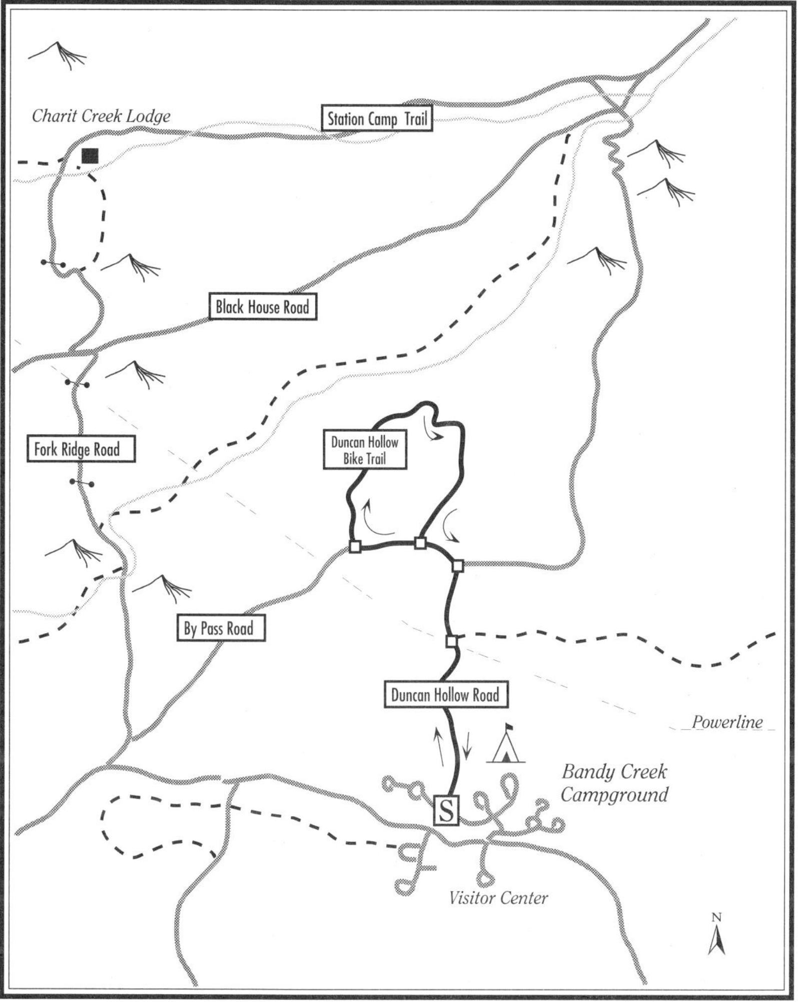

MAP KEY

Bike Route.........................

Other Trail or Road...........

Direction of Travel................

Start/Finish........................ S

Milepost.............................. □

Public Land.....................

Other Land.....................

Recreation/Camping Area....

Major Mountain........

River, Lake, or Stream.....

Forest Service Rd. #.................. 419

Road or Trail Name...... Thompson Loop

Foot Travel Only.............

Timber Cut or Clearing..

1600'
1300'

Elevation Change

Norris

The Norris Watershed holds an assortment of well maintained and well marked trails. Many are short connector trails and any number of loop combinations exist. The outer loop described here should get you off to a good start.

Start/Finish

Take US 441 north of Norris to Lower Clear Creek Road. Turn right past the grist mill and go 0.8 miles. The start is behind the pump station.

Trail Configuration

Loop

Surface

Single track (4WD) • 8 miles
Gravel road • 0.6 miles

Highlights

4 WD use, horse use, rocky, rolling hills, mud holes, lots of turns

Total Distance

8.6 miles

Time Allowance

Beginner • 2.5 hours
Intermediate • 1.75 hours
Advanced • 1.25 hours

Mileposts

- **From start–** ride up High Point Trail.
- **Mile 0.9–** turn right on Racoon Run Trail.
- **Mile 1.6–** White Pine Trail crosses. Bear hard right.
- **Mile 1.8–** just past gate, turn right on Red Hill Trail.
- **Mile 2.4–** turn right on Upper Clear Creek Road.
- **Mile 2.7–** turn left on Clear Creek Trail.
- **Mile 3.2–** Belmont Trail enters from left. Bear right.
- **Mile 3.6–** East Ridge Trail enters from right. Bear left.
- **Mile 4.1–** turn left on Boundary Trail just before house.
- **Mile 4.9–** turn left on Upper Clear Creek Road at barn.
- **Mile 5.2–** turn right on High Point Trail.
- **Mile 7.6–** turn right on Freeway Trail.
- **Mile 7.8–** turn left on Ridge Crest Trail (steep downhill).
- **Mile 8.6–** turn right on High Point Road to finish.

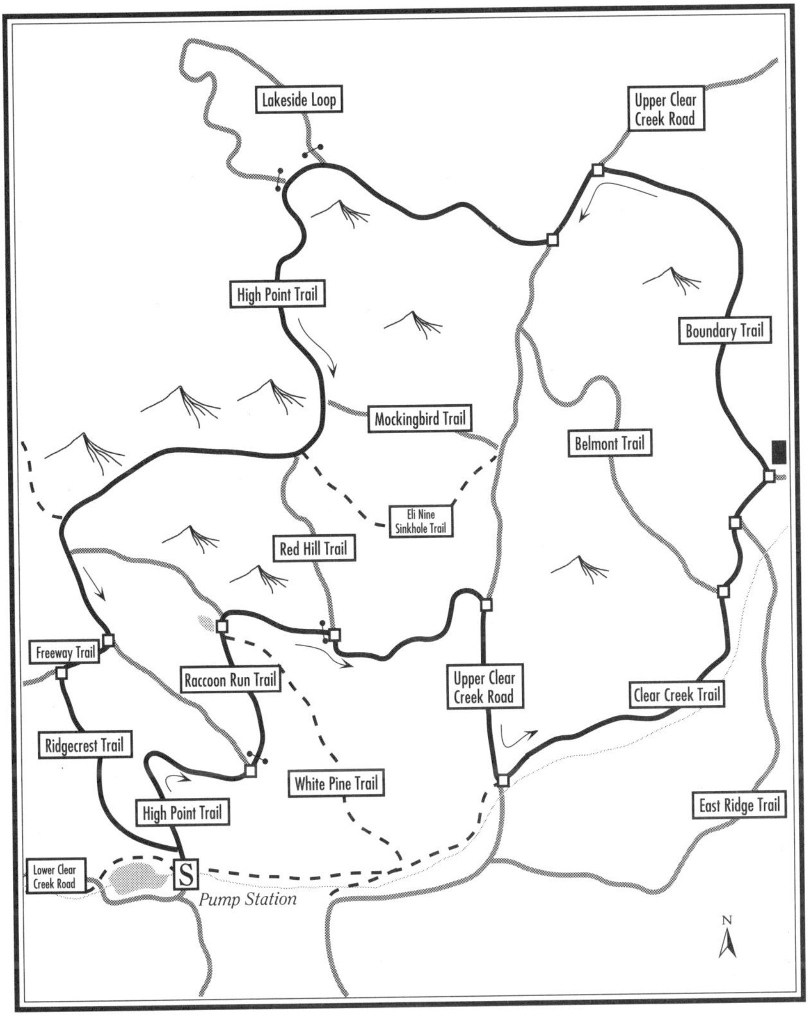

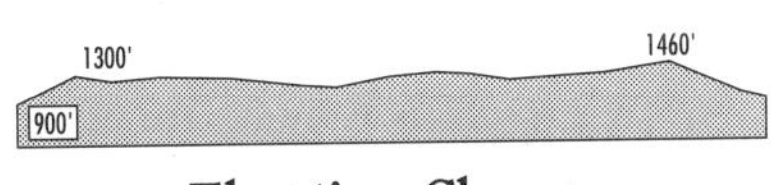

MAP KEY

Bike Route.......................

Other Trail or Road..........

Direction of Travel...............

Start/Finish...................... S

Milepost..............................

Public Land....................

Other Land.......................

Recreation/Camping Area....

Major Mountain........

River, Lake, or Stream.....

Forest Service Rd. #.................. 419

Road or Trail Name...... Thompson Loop

Foot Travel Only.............

Timber Cut or Clearing..

1300'   1460'
900'

Elevation Change

Chimney Rocks

After a good warmup in the rolling farmland of Houston Valley, you'll ascend the ridge of Pine Mountain. A grassy trail runs along this knife-like spine. The Chimney Rocks Trail is a beautiful stretch of twisting single track with unbelievable views of the French Broad River.

Start/Finish

Houston Valley Campground on TN 107, south of Greeneville.

Trail Configuration

Loop

Surface

Single track • 3.6 miles
Gravel road • 5.3 miles
Pavement • 4.6 miles

Highlights

Excellent views, rock bluffs, horse use, switchbacks, steep pitches

Total Distance

13.5 miles

Time Allowance

Beginner • 3.5 hours
Intermediate • 2.5 hours
Advanced • 1.75 hours

Mileposts

- **From start–** ride north on TN 107.
- **Mile 4.2–** Pine Spring Baptist Church. Turn right on FS 154.
- **Mile 6.1–** Lone Pine Gap. Turn right up gated road. A short distance up this seeded road, Paint Mountain Trail exits to the left. Stay on the seeded road as it climbs to the top of the ridge. It's marked with **yellow diamond blazes**.
- **Mile 7.2–** trail forks. Bear left on horse trail up steep hill.
- **Mile 7.4–** FS 54B enters left. Follow horse trail along left side of ridge.
- **Mile 7.6–** bear left on Chimney Rocks Trail **(yellow blazes)**.
- **Mile 9.7–** after crossing overgrown field, turn right on FS 209C at the railroad tracks.
- **Mile 11.4–** turn right on FS 209.
- **Mile 13.2–** turn left on TN 107 and ride 0.3 miles to finish.

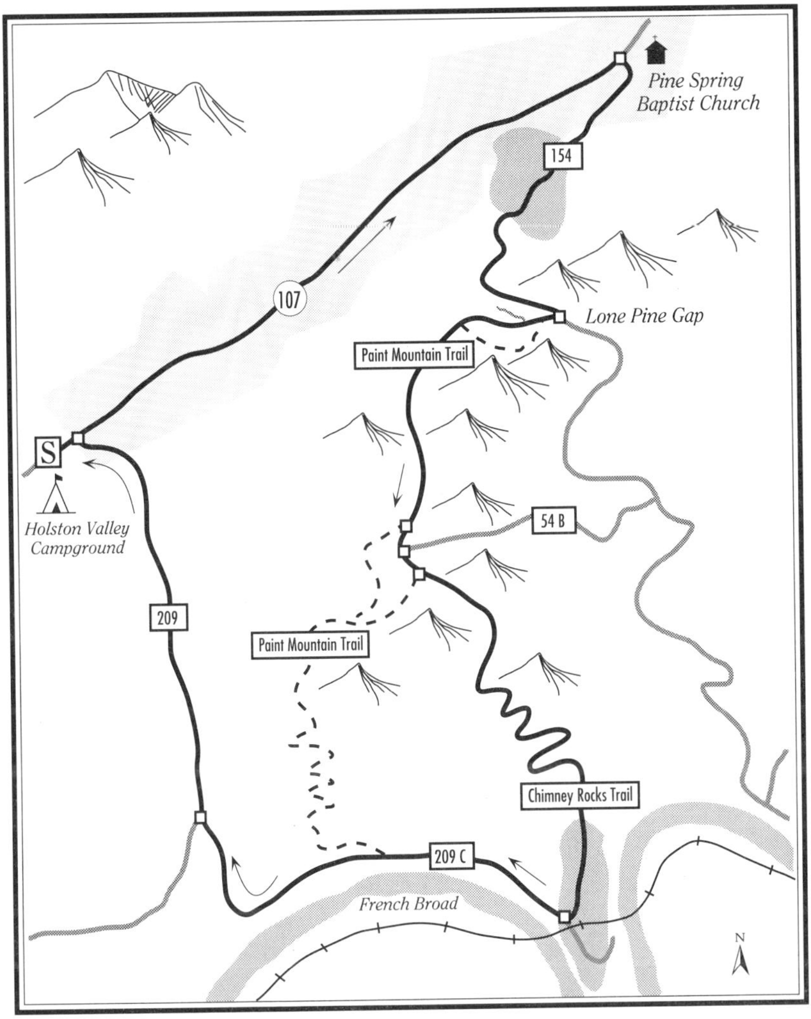

MAP KEY

Bike Route......................

Other Trail or Road...........

Direction of Travel...............

Start/Finish........................ S

Milepost................................. □

Public Land.....................

Other Land......................

Recreation/Camping Area....

Major Mountain........

River, Lake, or Stream.....

Forest Service Rd. #.................. 419

Road or Trail Name...... Thompson Loop

Foot Travel Only.............

Timber Cut or Clearing..

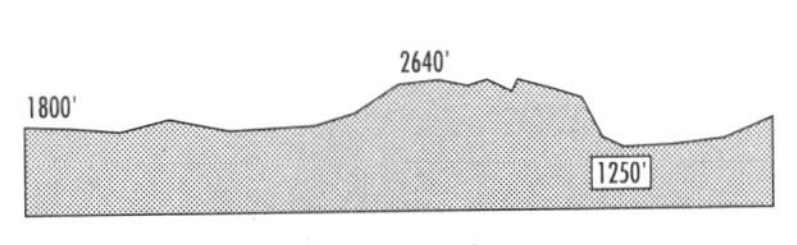

Elevation Change

38

14

Paint Rock

Casual pedaling alongside the cascades and waterfalls of Paint Creek makes for an easy beginning. Soon you'll arrive at Paint Rock, a huge bluff overlooking the French Broad River. Then it's a steady climb to Lone Pine Gap before you cruise back through Houston Valley's scenic rolling farmland.

Start/Finish

Paint Creek Campground, off TN 70 south of Greeneville.

Trail Configuration

Loop

Surface

Gravel road • 10.8 miles
Pavement • 2.8 miles

Highlights

Waterfalls, picnic areas, Paint Rock, French Broad River, mountain farms, views

Total Distance

13.6 miles

Time Allowance

Beginner • 2.5 hours
Intermediate • 2 hours
Advanced • 1.25 hours

Mileposts

- **From start**– ride downstream beside Paint Creek on FS 41.
- **Mile 5.0**– FS 54 turns off to the right. Paint Rock is just across bridge to the left. Go to the rock and then turn back and ride up FS 54.
- **Mile 8.2**– Lone Pine Gap and top of long hill climb.
- **Mile 10.1**– turn right on TN 107.
- **Mile 11.5**– turn right on Rollins Chapel Road.
- **Mile 12**– turn right toward Paint Creek Campground.
- **Mile 13.6**– finish.

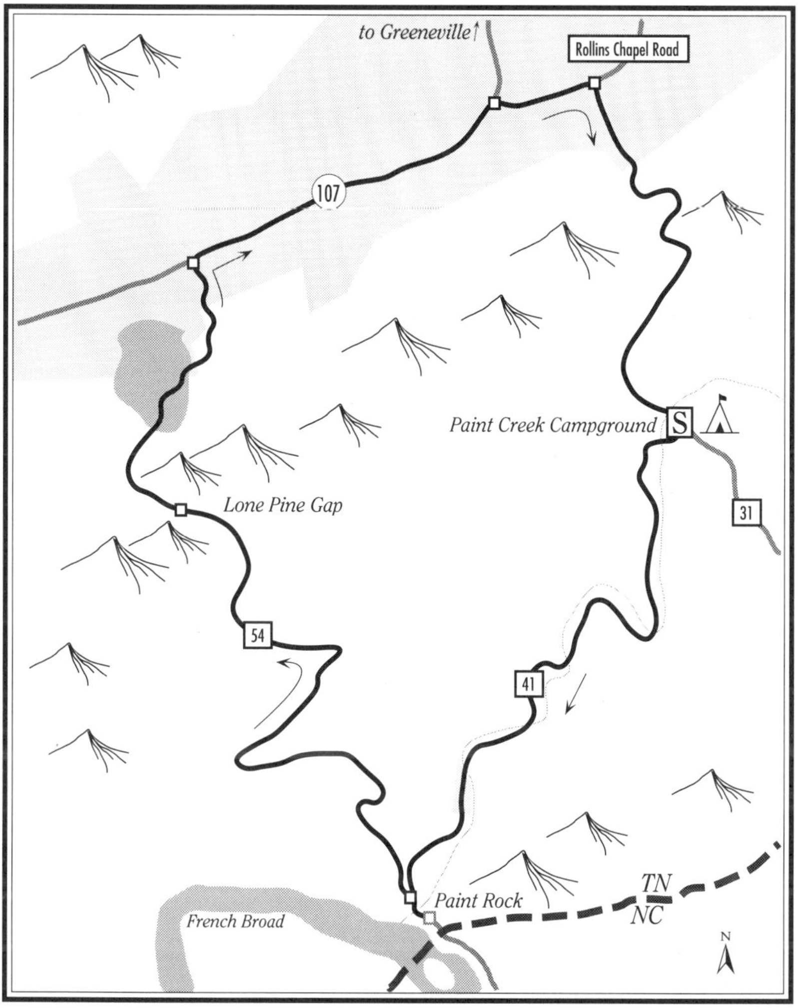

MAP KEY

Bike Route......................

Other Trail or Road..........

Direction of Travel...............

Start/Finish............................ S

Milepost.................................. □

Public Land.....................

Other Land.....................

Recreation/Camping Area....

Major Mountain........

River, Lake, or Stream.....

Forest Service Rd. #................. 419

Road or Trail Name...... Thompson Loop

Foot Travel Only.............

Timber Cut or Clearing..

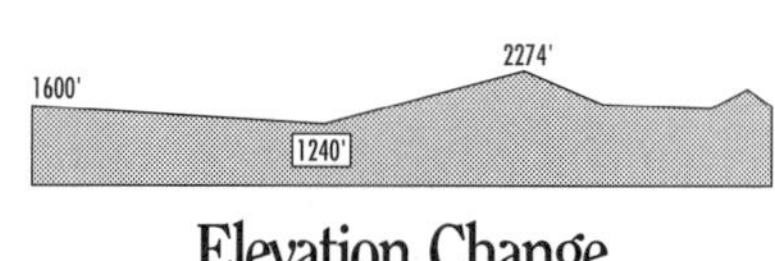

Elevation Change

Poplar Cove

You'll find this to be a short but difficult trail with multiple stream crossings. The last bit of the climb through the cove is very steep and rocky, but at the gap the trail settles into fairly decent downhill single track. Look out for horses.

Start/Finish

Horse Creek Recreation Area, off TN 107, south of Greeneville.

Trail Configuration

Loop

Surface

Single track • 3 miles
Gravel road • 1.7 miles
Pavement • 0.3 miles

Highlights

4WD use, heavy horse use, stream crossings, pushing required on rocky, steep section, waterfall side hike

Total Distance

5 miles

Time Allowance

Beginner • 3 hours
Intermediate • 1.75 hours
Advanced • 1 hour

Mileposts

- **From start–** ride upstream beside Horse Creek on 4WD FS 5094-2.
- **Mile 1–** take right fork at top of hill.
- **Mile 1.1–** 4WD road ends. Cross stream onto Poplar Cove Trail which is marked with **yellow diamond blazes.** Leave your bike here for a hike up the stream to the waterfall.
- **Mile 1.6–** Sarvis Cove Trail enters from left. Bear right up hill on Poplar Cove Trail and ride/push up and over gap.
- **Mile 2.1–** turn right on Jenning's Creek Trail.
- **Mile 2.9–** Little Jenning's Creek Trail enters from left. Bear right across stream.
- **Mile 3–** Old Forge Campground. Bear right on FS 331.
- **Mile 4.7–** turn right on paved FS 94.
- **Mile 5–** finish.

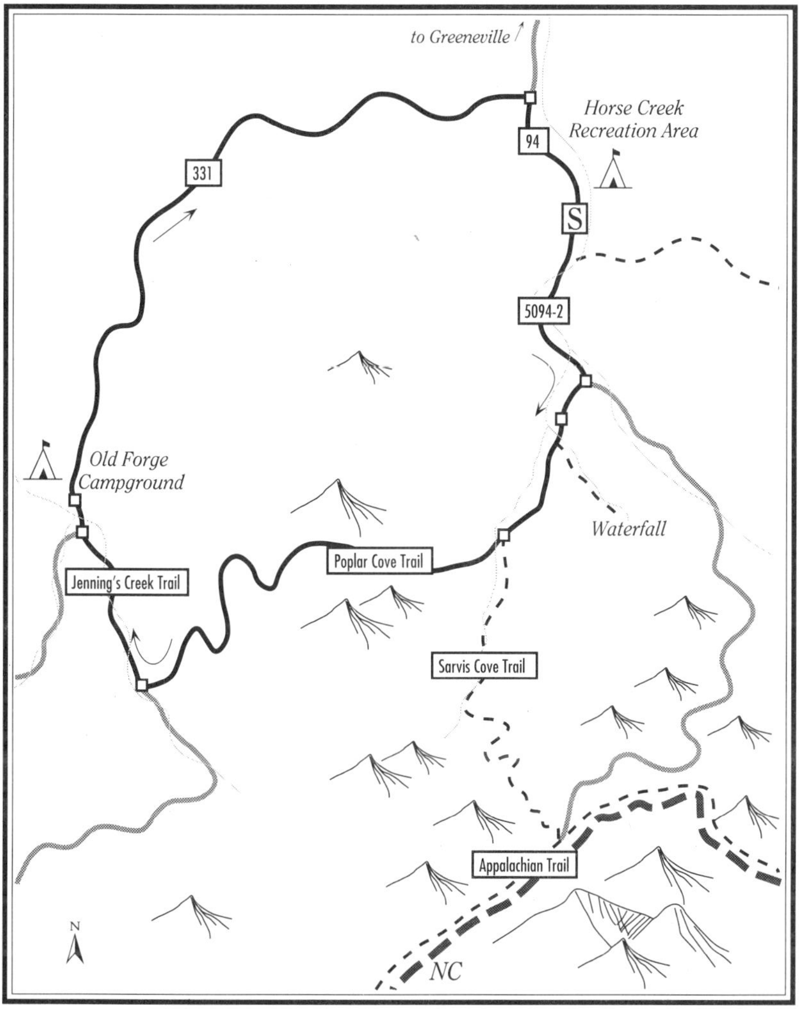

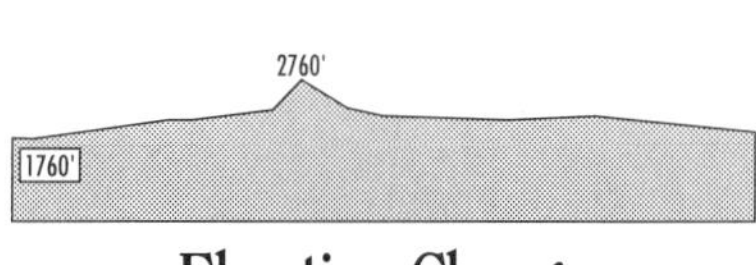

MAP KEY

Bike Route......................

Other Trail or Road...........

Direction of Travel...............

Start/Finish........................... S

Milepost..................................

Public Land....................

Other Land.....................

Recreation/Camping Area....

Major Mountain........

River, Lake, or Stream.....

Forest Service Rd. #.................. 419

Road or Trail Name...... Thompson Loop

Foot Travel Only............

Timber Cut or Clearing..

2760'

1760'

Elevation Change

Buffalo Mountain

The network of trails awaiting the cyclist on Buffalo Mountain can be very confusing, but this is probably the easiest route to follow. You'll find the ride up a bit of a grunt, but the fast, banking descent to the bottom makes it well worth the effort.

Start/Finish

From Erwin go 4.1 miles south on TN 81. Turn right on Arnold Road and go 1.9 miles. Turn right on Dry Creek Road and go 5.8 miles to Buffalo Mountain ATV trail head parking. Start here.

Trail Configuration

Loop

Surface

Single/double track • 6 miles
Pavement • 0.6 miles

Highlights

ATV use, crosses private land, high banked turns, rocky downhill, views, long climb

Total Distance

6.6 miles

Time Allowance

Beginner • 2.5 hours
Intermediate • 1.5 hours
Advanced • 1 hour

Mileposts

- **From start**– turn right out of parking area onto Dry Creek Road.
- **Mile 0.6**– turn right around gate onto double track. Bear left up the mountain.
- **Mile 4.1**– the trail crosses a gas pipeline. Bear right in the clear area on the trail that follows the pipeline and then left into the woods, just before the pipeline goes down a very steep hill.
- **Mile 4.2**– turn right onto Buffalo Mountain ATV Trail. It's marked with **blue blazes** and known to locals as the Blue Trail.
- **Mile 6.6**– finish.

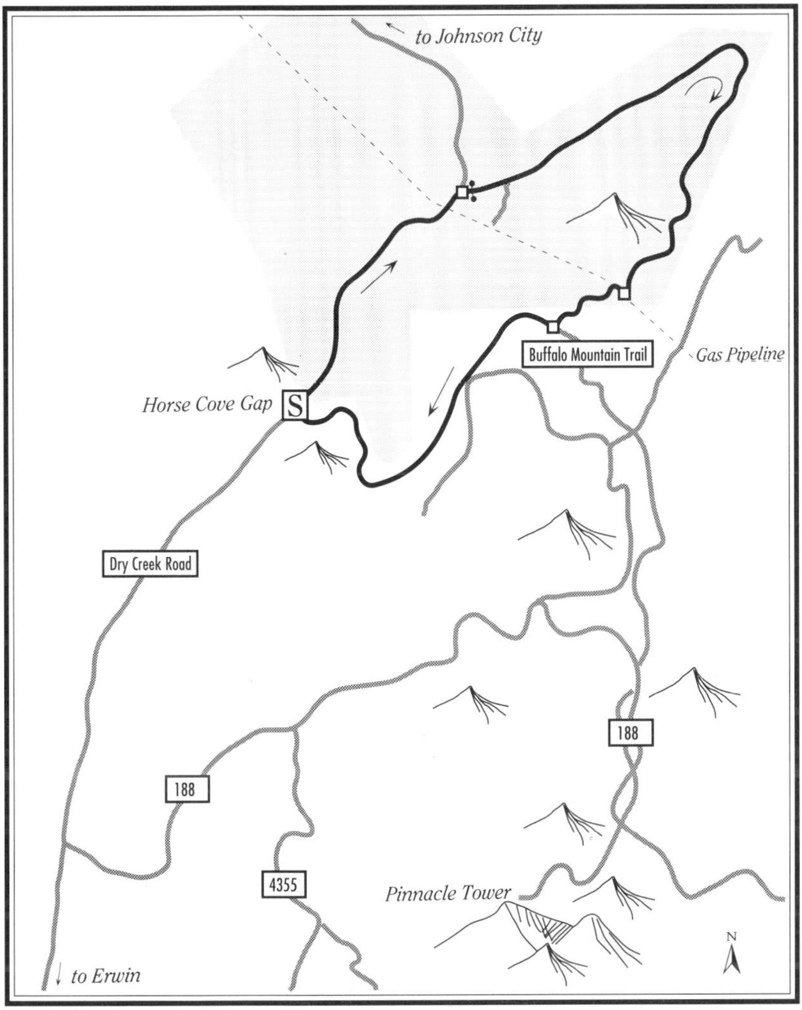

MAP KEY

Bike Route........................

Other Trail or Road...........

Direction of Travel................

Start/Finish............................ S

Milepost..................................... □

Public Land.....................

Other Land.......................

Recreation/Camping Area.... ⛺

Major Mountain........

River, Lake, or Stream.....

Forest Service Rd. #................ 419

Road or Trail Name...... Thompson Loop

Foot Travel Only.............

Timber Cut or Clearing..

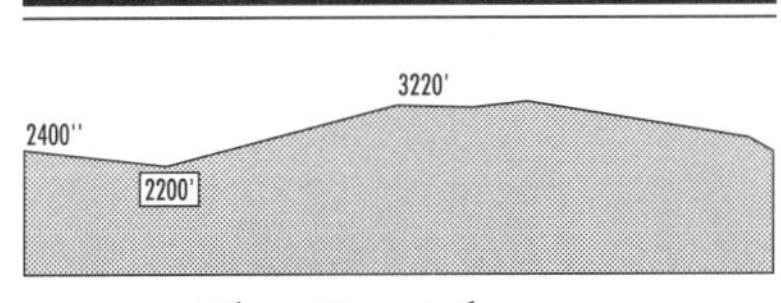

Elevation Change

Pinnacle Tower

Once atop this fire tower, you can see Erwin, Johnson City and the Blue Ridge. The view is simply great. Keep it in mind as you make the long climb to the top. Then hold on to your socks for the banking, swooping ride to the bottom.

Start/Finish

From Erwin go 4.1 miles south on TN 81. Turn right on Arnold Road and go 1.9 miles. Turn right on Dry Creek Road, go 5.8 miles to Buffalo Mountain ATV trail head parking. Start here.

Trail Configuration

Loop with extension

Surface

Single track • 3.7 miles
Gravel road • 6.9 miles
Pavement • 1.9 miles

Highlights

ATV use, lookout tower, high banked turns, rocky in places, some very technical sections, long climb

Total Distance

12.5 miles

Time Allowance

Beginner • 4 hours
Intermediate • 2.5 hours
Advanced • 1.75 hours

Mileposts

- **From start–** turn left onto Dry Creek Road.
- **Mile 1.9–** turn left onto FS 188 past gate.
- **Mile 4.1–** turn left up mountain at road fork.
- **Mile 5.4–** road forks. Turn right.
- **Mile 5.8–** Buffalo Mountain Trail enters from left.
- **Mile 7.3–** Pinnacle Mountain fire tower. Turn around and return to milepost 5.8.
- **Mile 8.8–** turn right on Buffalo Mountain Trail. It's marked with **blue blazes** and you will follow it all the way down to the finish. Numerous roads and trails will cross.
- **Mile 12.5–** finish.

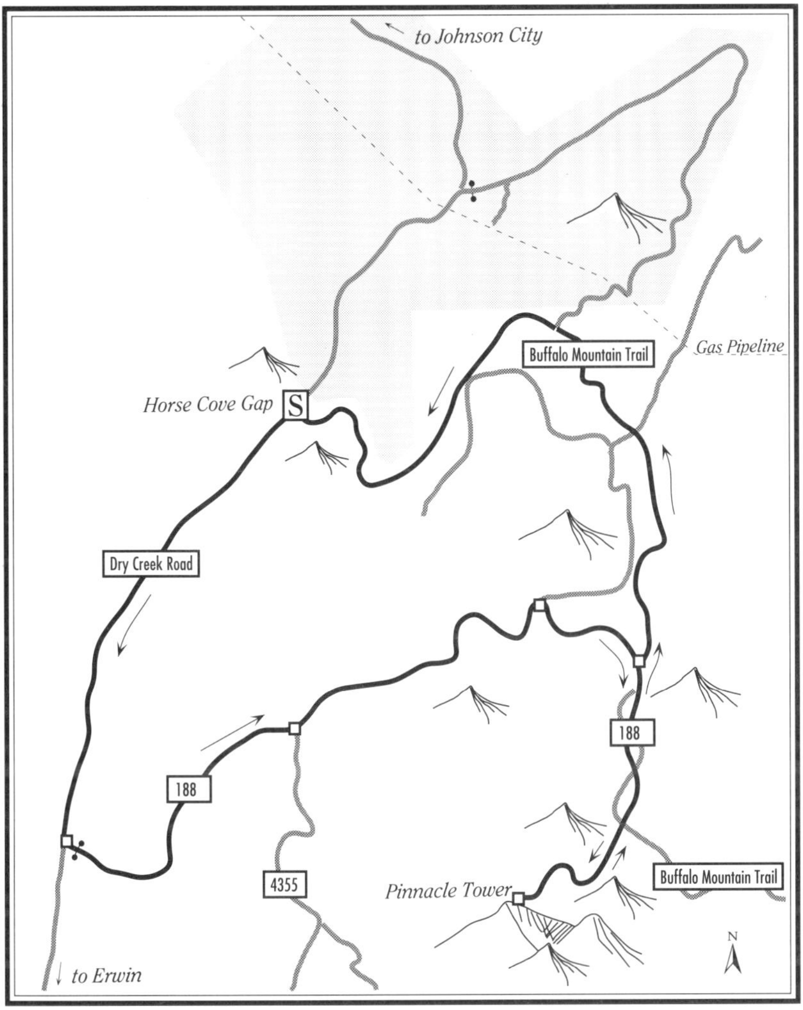

MAP KEY

Bike Route........................

Other Trail or Road..........

Direction of Travel................

Start/Finish............................ S

Milepost....................................

Public Land.......................

Other Land.......................

Recreation/Camping Area....

Major Mountain........

River, Lake, or Stream.....

Forest Service Rd. #.................. 419

Road or Trail Name...... Thompson Loop

Foot Travel Only.............

Timber Cut or Clearing..

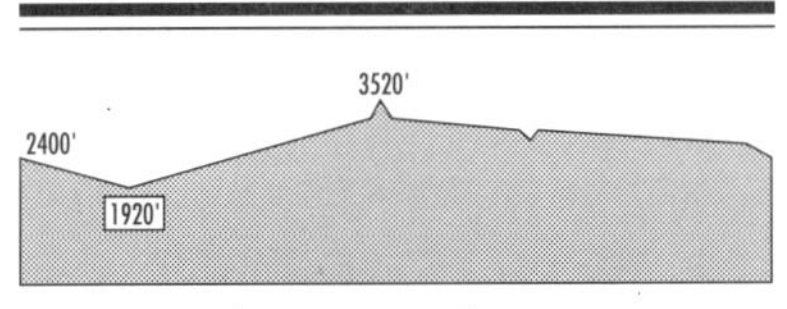

Elevation Change

MOST DIFFICULT TRAILS

18– Citico Creek • 22.6 Miles
19– Big Island • 11 Miles
20– Charit Creek Lodge • 13.5 Miles
21– North White Oak • 18 Miles
22– Hurricane Gap • 15 Miles
23– Viking Mountain • 16.1 Miles
24– Horse Creek • 7 Miles
25– McQueen Gap • 20.9 Miles

Citico Creek

In the spring of 1994 severe flooding ravaged the Citico Creek gorge. Trees were piled on top of bridges, much of the road was turned into a temporary riverbed and landslides left only very narrow passages. How long this damage will remain, no one knows. This route takes you high in the mountains before returning alongside the now calm Citico Creek.

Start/Finish

Indian Boundary Recreation Area Campground entrance, north of Tellico Plains on TN 165.

Trail Configuration

Loop

Surface

Single track/4WD • 11.6 miles
Gravel road • 10 miles
Pavement • 1 mile

Highlights

Washouts, landslides, timbercuts, very technical sections, views

Total Distance

22.6 miles

Time Allowance

Beginner • 6 hours
Intermediate • 4.5 hours
Advanced • 3 hours

Mileposts

- **From start**– ride back out paved road towards TN 165.
- **Mile 1**– turn right on FS 35.
- **Mile 1.6**– turn right on FS 284.
- **Mile 3.2**– turn right on FS 2033.
- **Mile 3.8**– road splits three ways. Take middle 4WD road.
- **Mile 5.4**– just before second meadow, turn right downhill.
- **Mile 8.0**– timbercut. Go around gate to left.
- **Mile 8.5**– go around gate and turn right on FS 5003.
- **Mile 9.7**– road forks. Take right fork out past gate.
- **Mile 12.5**– go around gate then take sharp right downhill.
- **Mile 15.4**– go around gate and turn right on FS 35-1.
- **Mile 18.8**– Doublecamp Campground. Bear right on 35-1.
- **Mile 20.3**– turn right up steep hill on FS 35-1.
- **Mile 22.6**– finish.

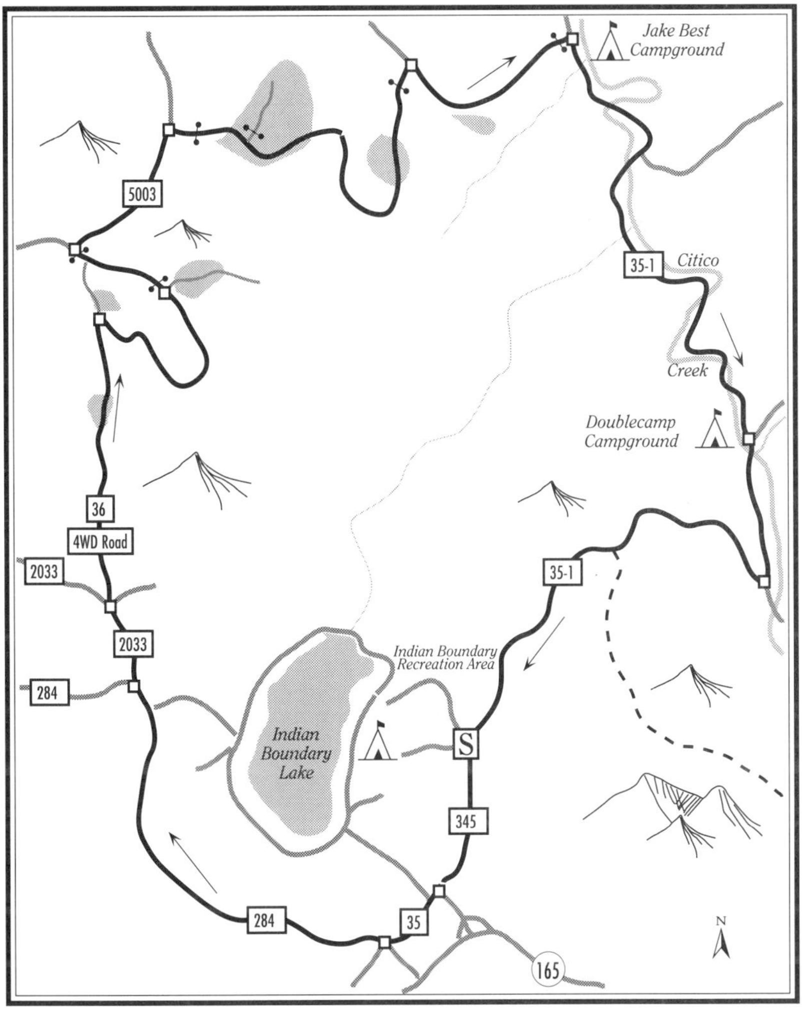

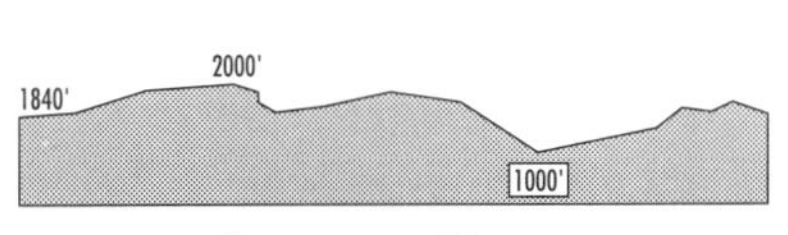

Map labels:

- Jake Best Campground
- 5003
- 35-1 Citico
- Creek
- Doublecamp Campground
- 36
- 4WD Road
- 2033
- 2033
- 284
- 35-1
- Indian Boundary Recreation Area
- Indian Boundary Lake
- S
- 345
- 284
- 35
- 165
- N

MAP KEY

Bike Route......................

Other Trail or Road..........

Direction of Travel............... →

Start/Finish........................... S

Milepost.................................... □

Public Land.....................

Other Land.....................

Recreation/Camping Area....

Major Mountain........

River, Lake, or Stream.....

Forest Service Rd. #................. 419

Road or Trail Name...... Thompson Loop

Foot Travel Only.............

Timber Cut or Clearing..

Elevation Change

1840' 2000' 1000'

19

Big Island

An extreme ride that'll throw the book at you. The first 3.5 miles are on beautiful rolling single track, but then the bottom drops out. A *very* steep sandstone staircase descent, riddled with rocks (it *is* ridable), takes you to the edge of the Big South Fork. Here you have to think like a horse and slog through a number of mud bogs and sand pits. You'll finish with a four mile climb.

Start/Finish

Station Camp East Trailhead, Big South Fork NRA. Go west from Oneida on TN 297. At Terry & Terry Store follow Station Camp Road 4.3 miles to the trailhead parking area.

Trail Configuration

Loop

Surface

Single track • 7.2 miles
Gravel road • 3.8 miles

Highlights

Heavy horse use, sand, mud bogs, cabin, chimney rocks, river views

Total Distance

11 miles

Time Allowance

Beginner • not recommended
Intermediate • 3.5 hours
Advanced • 1.75 hours

Mileposts

- **From start**– ride out Big Island Loop Trail.
- **Mile 0.5**– gravel road enters from left. Bear right.
- **Mile 1.2**– start Big Island loop by turning right.
- **Mile 2.6**– cross woods road.
- **Mile 3.5**– turn left past gate down *very* steep hill.
- **Mile 4.5**– Big Island river crossing. Turn left, upstream.
- **Mile 4.9**– log cabin.
- **Mile 7.2**– Station Camp river crossing. Turn left on Station Camp Road and climb out of gorge.
- **Mile 11**– finish.

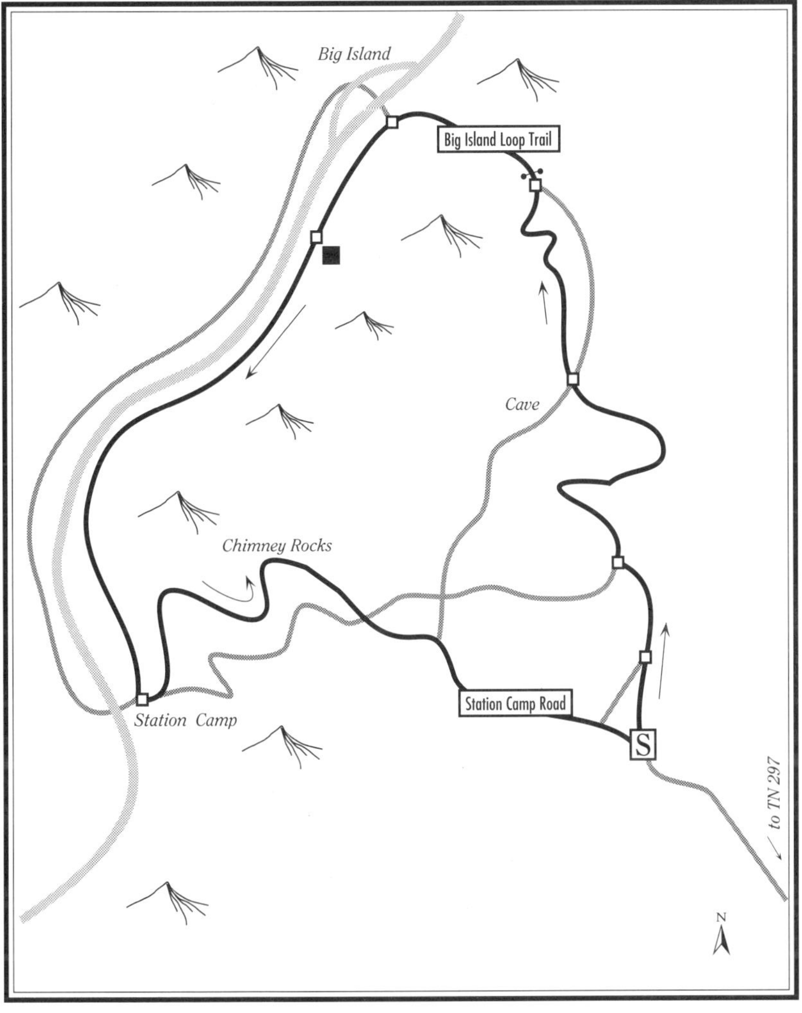

MAP KEY

Bike Route.........................

Other Trail or Road...........

Direction of Travel................

Start/Finish.............................. S

Milepost...............................

Public Land......................

Other Land......................

Recreation/Camping Area....

Major Mountain........

River, Lake, or Stream.....

Forest Service Rd. #.................. 419

Road or Trail Name...... Thompson Loop

Foot Travel Only.............

Timber Cut or Clearing..

1500'

800'

Elevation Change

20

Charit Creek Lodge

This difficult loop takes you by an impressive log lodge in the wilderness. The people who stay here arrive on foot, horseback or fat tire only. You'll also encounter multiple stream crossings, some rock caves, and at least one mandatory push up a steep, rocky trail.

Start/Finish

Bandy Creek Visitor Center, Big South Fork National Recreation Area near Oneida.

Trail Configuration

Loop

Surface

Single track/4WD • 7.8 miles
Gravel road • 5.5 miless
Pavement • 0.2 miles

Highlights

Heavy horse use, deep sand areas, mud bogs, washouts, stream crossings, caves, steep hills

Total Distance

13.5 miles

Time Allowance

Beginner • 5 hours
Intermediate • 3 hours
Advanced • 2 hours

Mileposts

- **From start**– ride west out Bandy Creek Road.
- **Mile 1.2**– just past county line, turn right on 4WD road.
- **Mile 1.4**– By Pass Road enters from right. Bear left.
- **Mile 2**– trails jct. Turn left past gate down steep hill. All horse trails are marked with a **yellow horse head**.
- **Mile 3.8**– turn left on Black House Road.
- **Mile 3.9**– turn right on gravel road.
- **Mile 4.1**– trail head parking lot. Take horse trail to left.
- **Mile 5.2**– Charit Creek Lodge and Hostel. Trail continues around left side of lodge and follows Station Camp Creek.
- **Mile 8.2**– at trail sign, turn right toward Bandy Creek.
- **Mile 8.4**– cross Laurel Fork and head up steep horse trail.
- **Mile 9.2**– Duncan Hollow Road. Take it to the finish.
- **Mile 13.5**– finish.

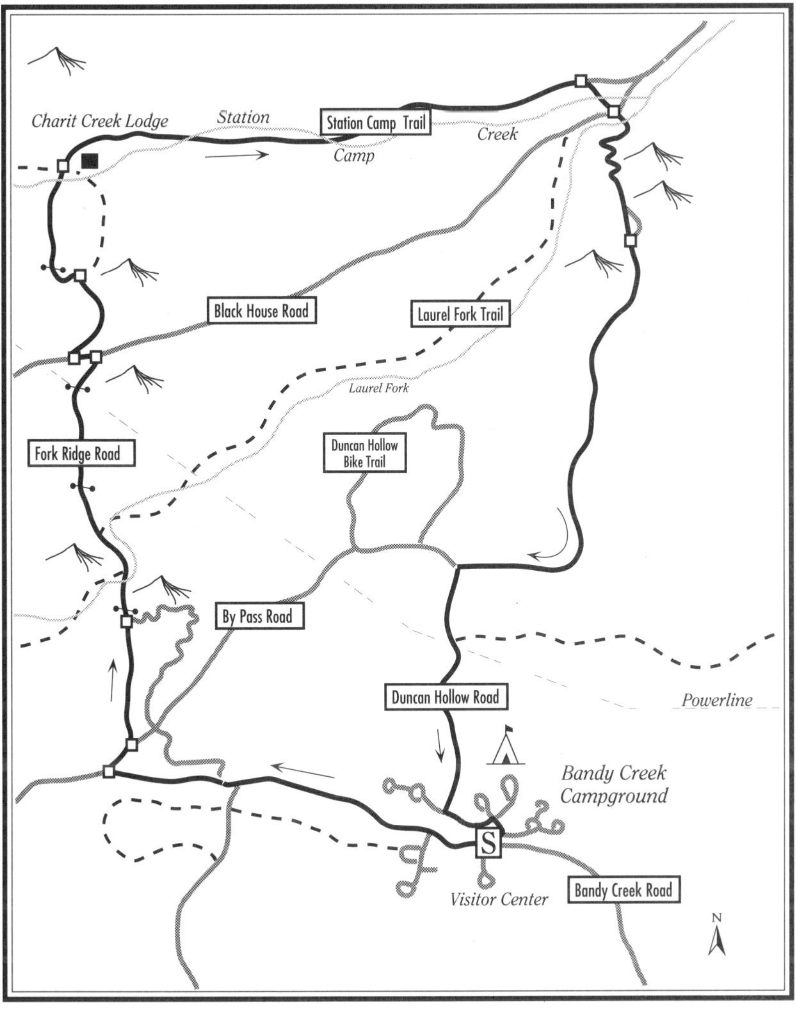

MAP KEY

Bike Route.........................

Other Trail or Road..........

Direction of Travel...............

Start/Finish........................... S

Milepost.............................. □

Public Land.......................

Other Land.......................

Recreation/Camping Area....

Major Mountain........

River, Lake, or Stream.....

Forest Service Rd. #................. 419

Road or Trail Name...... Thompson Loop

Foot Travel Only.............

Timber Cut or Clearing..

1600'
850'

Elevation Change

21

North White Oak

This long single track loop takes you out to a high overlook above White Oak Creek Gorge. There are numerous   short climbs as you wind and curve through the woods. You'll cross several small streams and a number of large mud bogs and sand pits.

Start/Finish

Bandy Creek Horse Camp, Big South Fork National Recreation Area west of Oneida off TN 297.

Trail Configuration

Loop

Surface

Single track • 15 miles
Gravel road • 0.1 miles
Pavement • 2.9 miles

Highlights

Heavy horse use, overlook, deep sand areas, mud bogs, washouts, small stream crossings

Total Distance

18 miles

Time Allowance

Beginner • 5 hours
Intermediate • 3.5 hours
Advanced • 2.25 hours

Mileposts

- **From start**– ride through horse camp onto North White Oak Loop Trail. Follow the **yellow horse head blazes**.
- **Mile 0.7**– there are some serious mud bogs to this point. Turn right at the fork.
- **Mile 1.4**– cross TN 297.
- **Mile 7**– trails jct. Turn right to overlook.
- **Mile 8.2**– turn-around area. It's a short hike to the overlook from here.
- **Mile 9.5**– back at trails jct. Turn right on horse trail.
- **Mile 14.5**– turn left on Leatherwood Road.
- **Mile 15**– turn right on gravel road.
- **Mile 15.1**– turn right on TN 297.
- **Mile 16.4**– turn left on Bandy Creek Road.
- **Mile 18**– finish.

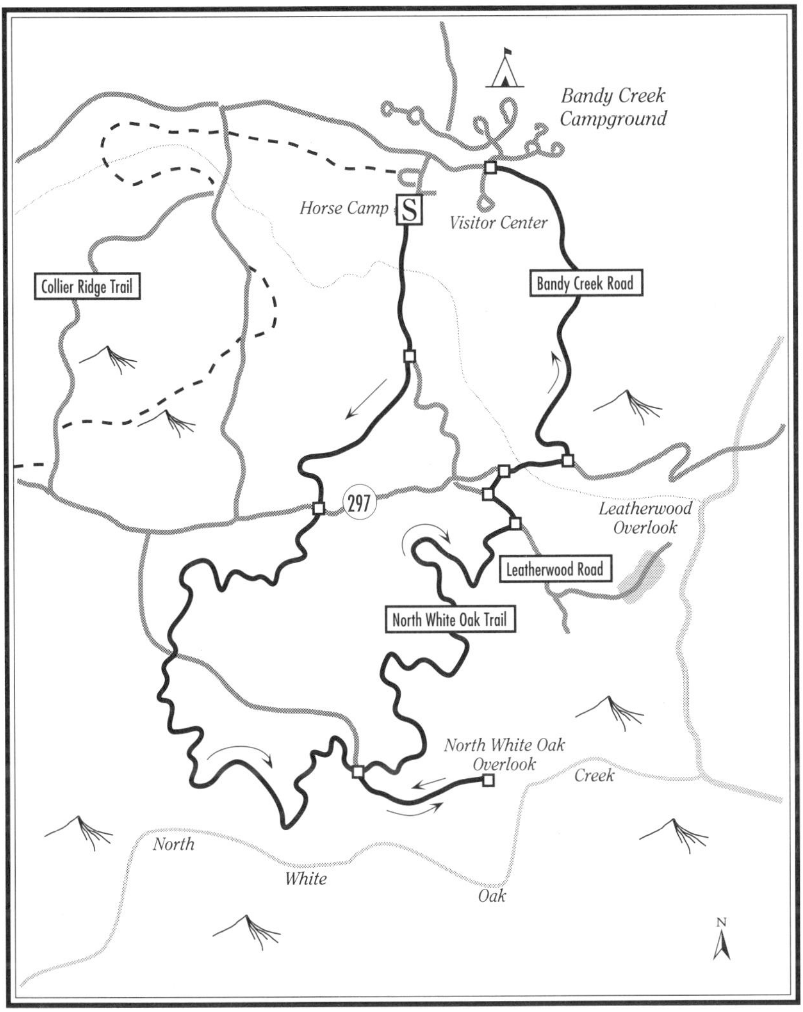

MAP KEY

Bike Route........................

Other Trail or Road...........

Direction of Travel............... →

Start/Finish............................ S

Milepost................................... □

Public Land........................

Other Land........................

Recreation/Camping Area....

Major Mountain........

River, Lake, or Stream.....

Forest Service Rd. #................. 419

Road or Trail Name...... Thompson Loop

Foot Travel Only.............

Timber Cut or Clearing..

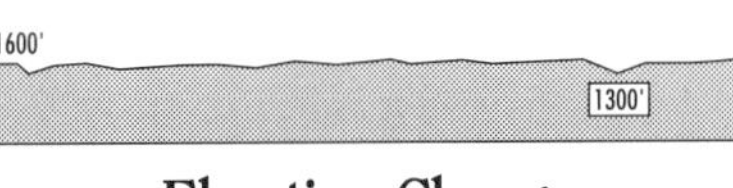

Elevation Change

◆ 22 ◆

Hurricane Gap

An excellent ride that takes you up through Hurricane Gap and across the Appalachian Trail to the Rich Mountain fire tower. Here you'll have excellent views of both Tennessee and North Carolina. The ride back down follows the state line. Make sure to stay on the main road or you may end up in the wrong state!

Start/Finish

From Paint Creek Campground, off TN 70 south of Greeneville, take FS 31 for 1.7 miles. Start at its intersection with FS 422A.

Trail Configuration

Loop with extension

Surface

Double track • 1.7 miles
Gravel road • 13.3 miles

Highlights

Lookout tower, one very steep downhill pitch, mud holes, 4WD use, timbercuts, state line

Total Distance

15 miles

Time Allowance

Beginner • 3.5 hours
Intermediate • 2.5 hours
Advanced • 1.75 hours

Mileposts

- **From start–** ride south on FS 31.
- **Mile 2.3–** FS 31B enters left. Stay on FS 31.
- **Mile 3.2–** Hurricane Gap and state line. Bear right.
- **Mile 3.3–** FS 422 enters right, Appalachian Trail crosses, and a gated road enters left. Ride uphill on FS 467A.
- **Mile 4.2–** Rich Mountain lookout tower. Turn around.
- **Mile 5.4–** turn left on FS 422.
- **Mile 10.6–** Jack's Branch Trail enters left. FS 422 becomes more of a four wheel drive road. Stay on FS 422.
- **Mile 11.2–** road forks. Bear right to stay in Tennessee.
- **Mile 12.3–** after steep downhill, turn right on FS 422A.
- **Mile 15–** finish.

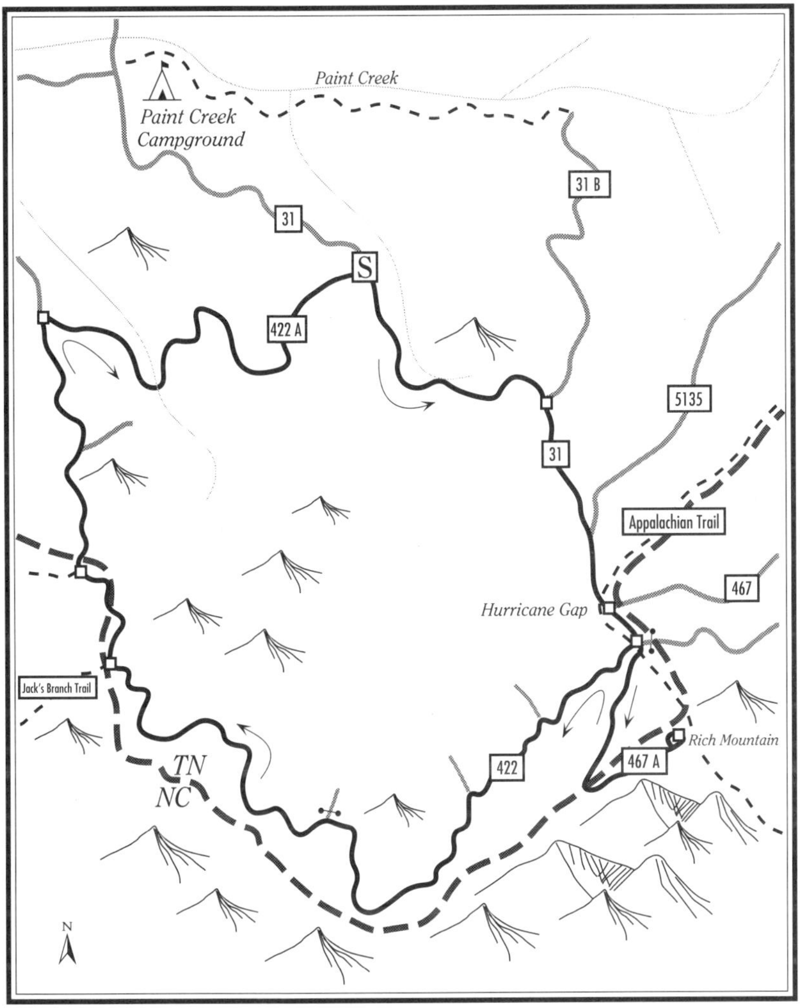

MAP KEY

Bike Route........................

Forest Service Rd. #................. 419

Other Trail or Road..........

Road or Trail Name...... Thompson Loop

Direction of Travel................

Foot Travel Only............

Start/Finish........................... S

Timber Cut or Clearing..

Milepost.....................................

Public Land.....................

Other Land.....................

Recreation/Camping Area....

Major Mountain........

River, Lake, or Stream.....

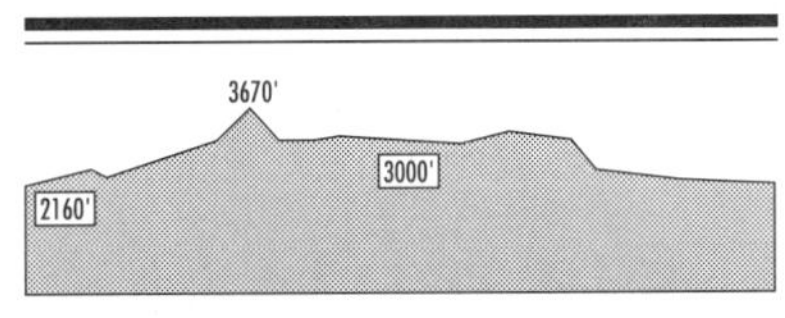

Elevation Change

Viking Mountain

This is a magnificent ride to a lookout tower and a modern-day ghost town in the sky—a vacation homes development gone broke. Be sure to tighten your brake cables for the single track descent.

Start/Finish

0.2 miles from the state line on TN 70 (NC 208) turn onto Viking Mountain Road. Drive 1.1 miles and start at Upper Paint Creek Church.

Trail Configuration

Loop with extension

Surface

Single track • 3 miles
Gravel road • 8.9 miles
Pavement • 4.2 miles

Highlights

Great views, Blackstack Cliffs, lookout tower, steep sections, horse use, 4WD use, state line, Jones Meadow

Total Distance

16.1miles

Time Allowance

Beginner • 5 hours
Intermediate • 3 hours
Advanced • 2.25 hours

Mileposts

- **From start–** ride up paved Viking Mountain Road.
- **Mile 0.4–** Green Mountain Road enters from the left.
- **Mile 4.5–** FS 358 enters left. Stay on Viking Mountain Road.
- **Mile 6.3–** Jones Meadow. Turn right and it's 0.7 miles to the lookout tower. Turn left and it's 0.3 miles to the cliff overlook. After exploring around, return the way you came up.
- **Mile 10.2–** turn right past gate on FS 358.
- **Mile 11–** road forks. Bear left toward Kennedy Cabin.
- **Mile 11.7–** just past gated road on left, turn left on Green Mountain Trail (**yellow diamond blazes**). This trail is inter-twined with another for half a mile. Follow either one.
- **Mile 14.7–** turn left on Green Mountain Road.
- **Mile 15.6–** turn right on Viking Mountain Road.
- **Mile 16.1–** finish.

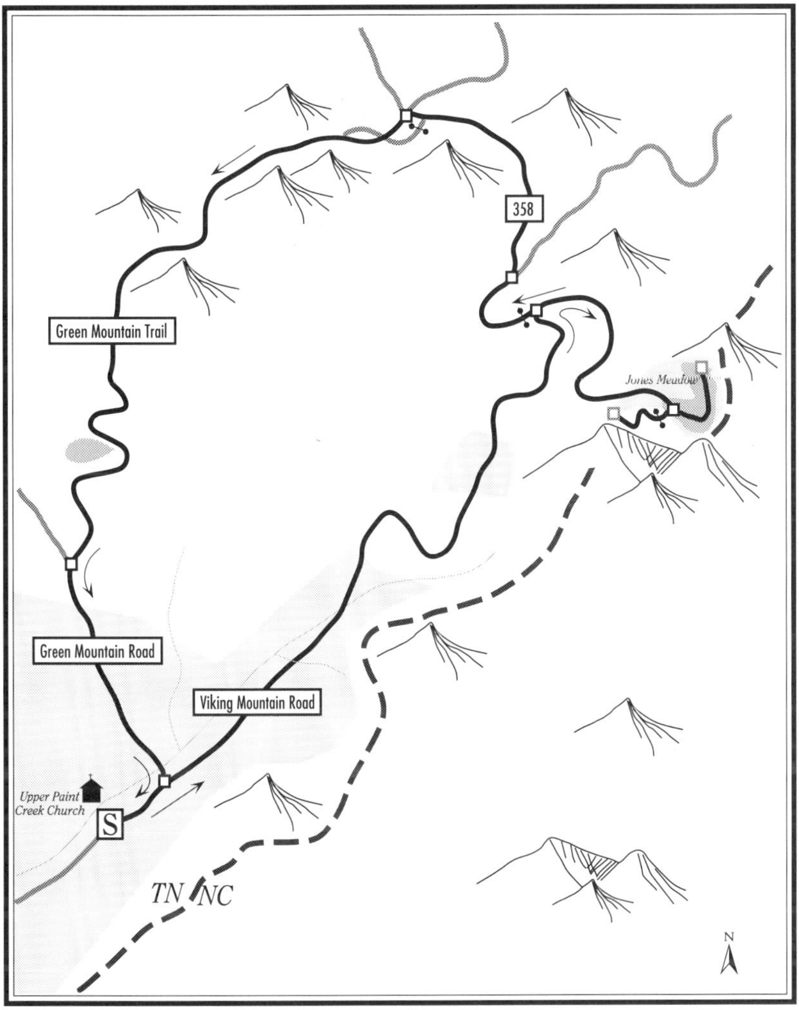

Green Mountain Trail

358

Jones Meadow

Green Mountain Road

Viking Mountain Road

Upper Paint
Creek Church

S

TN NC

N

MAP KEY

Bike Route........................

Other Trail or Road...........

Direction of Travel............... →

Start/Finish........................... S

Milepost................................... □

Public Land.....................

Other Land.....................

Recreation/Camping Area....

Major Mountain........

River, Lake, or Stream.....

Forest Service Rd. #................. 419

Road or Trail Name...... Thompson Loop

Foot Travel Only............

Timber Cut or Clearing..

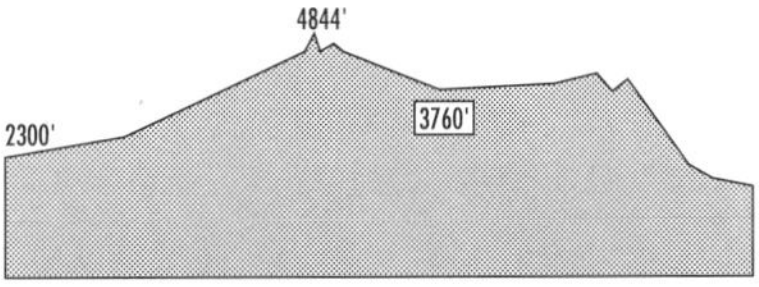

Elevation Change

Horse Creek

If you're in the mood for a super-steep, ridable hill climb with a great view at the top, here's one for you. This 4WD road climb will test your legs and your lungs and reward you with a super view of Greeneville, the Nolichucky River Valley and points beyond. Believe me, it's steep!

Start/Finish

Horse Creek Recreation Area, off TN 107, south of Greeneville.

Trail Configuration

Out-and-back

Surface

Double track • 7 miles

Highlights

4WD use, horse use, multiple stream crossings, views, steep

Total Distance

7 miles

Time Allowance

Beginner • 4 hours
Intermediate • 3 hours
Advanced • 2 hours

Mileposts

- **From start–** ride upstream beside Horse Creek on 4WD FS 5094-2.
- **Mile 1–** bear left uphill at fork.
- **Mile 3.1–** level turn-around area. A short side trail through the bushes leads to a spectacular cliff-top view. Continue up hill.
- **Mile 3.3–** gated road to left, bear right.
- **Mile 3.5–** road ends. Jct. Appalachian Trail and Sarvis Cove Trail. You can explore around on foot here, then return the way you came up.
- **Mile 7–** finish.

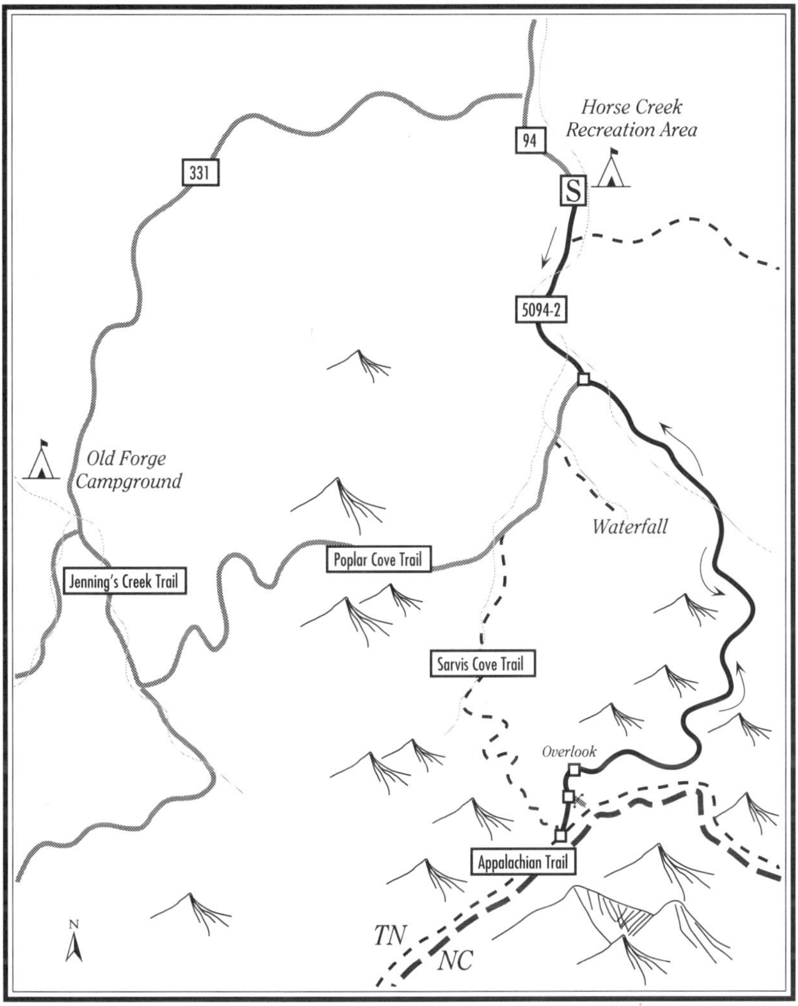

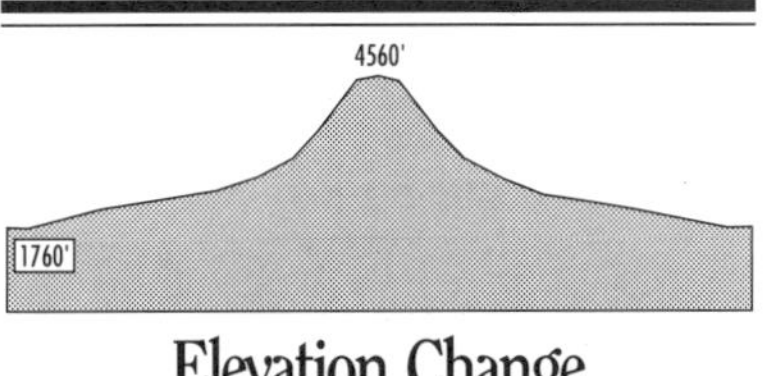

MAP KEY

Bike Route........................

Other Trail or Road..........

Direction of Travel...............

Start/Finish............................ S

Milepost...................................

Public Land.....................

Other Land.....................

Recreation/Camping Area....

Major Mountain........

River, Lake, or Stream.....

Forest Service Rd. #................. 419

Road or Trail Name...... Thompson Loop

Foot Travel Only.............

Timber Cut or Clearing..

4560'

1760'

Elevation Change

McQueen Gap

On this route, you ride almost to Virginia before turning up Holston Mountain to McQueen Gap just short of the Appalachian Trail. It's a wilderness ride, interrupted only briefly by the small mountain community of Offset. Be sure to allow plenty of time as there are several long climbs.

Start/Finish

From Bristol, take US 421 south 12.5 miles to FS 4002 on the left. Start at the gate.

Trail Configuration

Loop

Surface

Gravel road • 18.9 miles
Pavement • 2 miles

Highlights

Small streams, long climbs, spotty views, mountain community, short section of overgrown road

Total Distance

20.9 miles

Time Allowance

Beginner • 5 hours
Intermediate • 3.25 hours
Advanced • 2.25 hours

Mileposts

- **From start–** ride around gate and out FS 4002.
- **Mile 5.2–** go around gate and turn right on FS 32.
- **Mile 8.4–** road turns to pavement.
- **Mile 8.8–** roads junction at small community of Offset. Turn right on gravel FS 69.
- **Mile 12.0–** McQueen Gap. Just before top of ridge and Appalachian Trail crossing, turn right past gate on FS 4431. The road may be somewhat overgrown for the first few miles.
- **Mile 16.1–** gate. Road becomes much better here.
- **Mile 19.3–** ride around gate and turn right on US 421.
- **Mile 20.9–** finish.

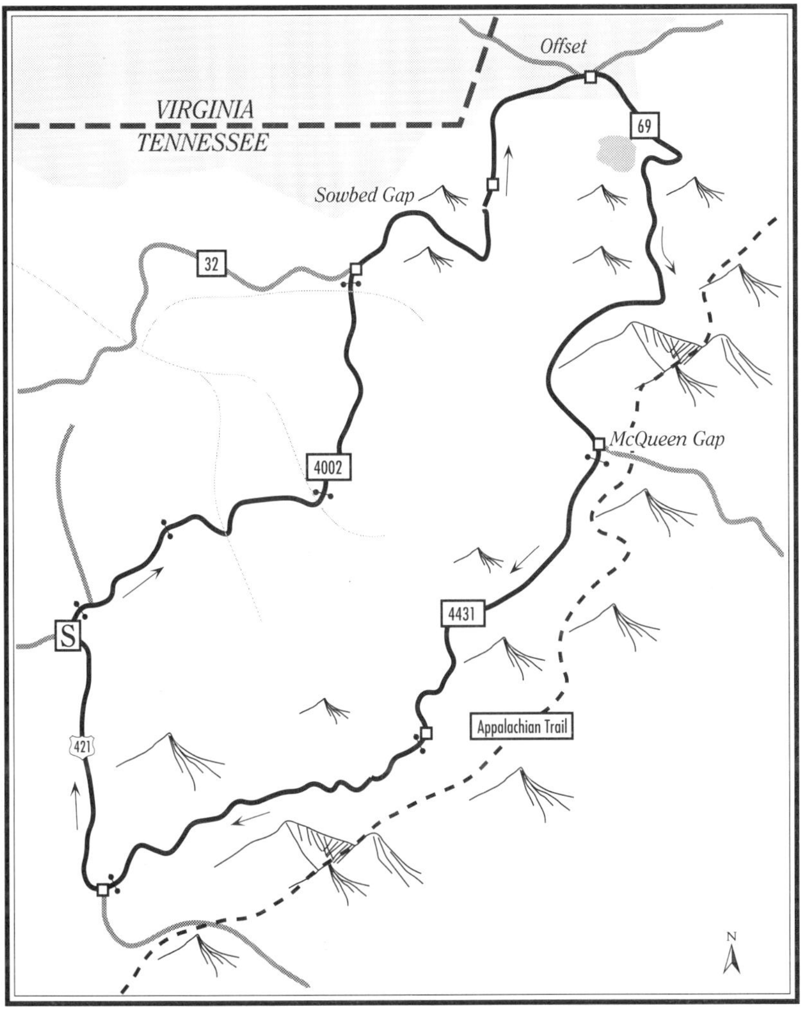

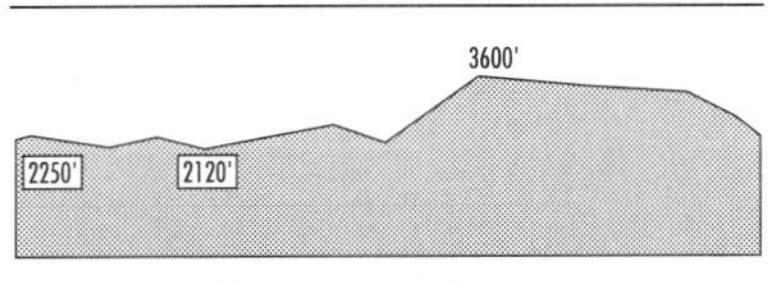

MAP KEY

Bike Route.....................

Other Trail or Road..........

Direction of Travel...............

Start/Finish............................ S

Milepost.....................................

Public Land.....................

Other Land.....................

Recreation/Camping Area....

Major Mountain........

River, Lake, or Stream.....

Forest Service Rd. #................. 419

Road or Trail Name...... Thompson Loop

Foot Travel Only............

Timber Cut or Clearing..

Elevation Change

3600'

2250' 2120'

Regional Information

Local Bike Resources
Lodging
Camping
Weather

Local Bike Resources

Knoxville Area

- **K. T.'s Bicycle Shop**
  4815 Clinton Hwy.
  Knoxville, TN 37912
  615/688-2223

- **Bike Zoo**
  1909 Cumberland Ave.
  Knoxville, TN 37916
  615/558-8455

- **West Hills Bicycle Center**
  1707 Cumberland Ave.
  Knoxville, TN 37916
  615/546-6667

- **River Sports Outfitters**
  2918 Sutherland Ave.
  Knoxville, TN 37919
  615/523-0066

Other Areas

- **Backwoods Adventures**
  327 Hwy 297
  Oneida, TN 37841
  615/569-9573

- **Piney Flats Bikes**
  5585 Hwy 11E
  Piney Flats, TN 37686
  615/538-9005

Lodging

Most of the rides in this book are close to towns or cities which have quite a few lodging establishments to choose from. Below is a list of chambers of commerce who can provide current information on lodging in the area of your choice.

- **Jamestown Chamber of Commerce**
  P.O. Box 496
  Jamestown, TN
  615/879-9948.

- **Oneida Chamber of Commerce**
  P.O. Box 4442
  Oneida, TN 37841
  615/569-6900

- **Bristol Chamber of Commerce**
  P.O. Box 519
  Bristol, TN/VA 24203-0519
  615/989-4850

- **Johnson City Chamber of Commerce**
  P.O. Box 180
  Johnson City, TN 37605
  615/461-8000

- **Greenville Chamber of Commerce**
  207 North Main
  Greenville, TN 37743
  615/638-4111

- **Cleveland/Bradley Chamber of Commerce**
  P.O. Box 2275
  Cleveland, TN 37320
  615/472-6587

Camping

Many of the rides in this book begin at or near a public campground. Except for Bandy Creek Campground which is located in the Big South Fork National Recreation Area (615/879-3625) and Panther Creek Campground which is located in Panther Creek State Park (615/587-7046), all are located in the Cherokee National Forest. These national forest campgrounds are generally open May through October and sites are taken on a first-come, first-served basis. Bandy Creek and Panther Creek are open year-round.

While different fees are charged at the different campgrounds, backcountry camping is permitted free of charge throughout the Cherokee National Forest (unless signs are posted otherwise) and at least 100 feet from any river, trail or road in the Big South Fork National Recreation Area.

For those interested in staying at the Charit Creek Lodge (access by foot, mountain bike or horseback only) contact: Charit Creek Lodge, Box 350, Gatlinburg, TN 37738, phone 615/429-5704.

Weather

Month	Average Temperature	Average Rainfall*
January	37°	5.0"
February	40°	4.5"
March	47°	6.0"
April	57°	4.5"
May	65°	4.5"
June	72°	4.5"
July	76°	5.5"
August	75°	4.0"
September	70°	4.0"
October	57°	3.0"
November	45°	4.0"
December	40°	5.0"

*All temperatures are fahrenheit. Above data is based on information provided by the National Climatic Data Center.

Notes

Notes

Notes

Notes

Notes

Notes